THE
WINTER PEOPLE

THE
WINTER PEOPLE

Joseph Bruchac

Dial Books  New York

Published by Dial Books
A division of Penguin Putnam Inc.
345 Hudson Street
New York, New York 10014
Copyright © 2002 by Joseph Bruchac
All rights reserved
Map and book design by Jasmin Rubero
Text set in Adobe Caslon
Printed in the U.S.A. on acid-free paper
1 3 5 7 9 10 8 6 4 2

Library of Congress Cataloging-in-Publication Data
Bruchac, Joseph, date.
The winter people / Joseph Bruchac.
p.   cm.
Summary: As the French and Indian War rages
in October of 1759, Saxso, a fourteen-year-old Abenaki boy,
pursues the English rangers who have attacked his
village and taken his mother and sisters hostage.
ISBN 0-8037-2694-5
1. United States—History—French and Indian
War, 1755-1763—Juvenile fiction. 2. Abenaki Indians—
Juvenile fiction. [1. United States—
History—French and Indian War, 1755-1763—Fiction.
2. Abenaki Indians—Fiction.
3. Indians of North America—Canada, Eastern—Fiction.
4. Coming of age—Fiction. 5. Quebec
(Quebec)—History—French and Indian War, 1755-1763—Fiction.
6. Canada—History—1755-1763—Fiction.] I. Title.
PZ7.B82816 Wi 2002   [Fic]—2002000338

This book is dedicated to the memory of
Stephen Laurent, Chief Homer St. Francis,
Wolf Song, Molly Keating, and to all those who
have gone but will never leave us.

Wli dogo Wôngan.

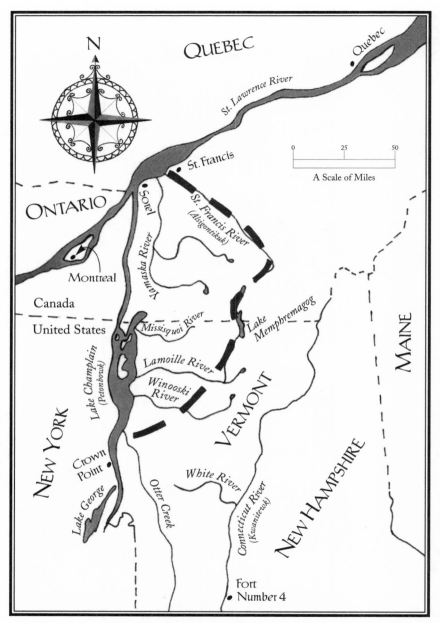

N

QUEBEC

St. Lawrence River

Quebec

0   25   50
A Scale of Miles

St. Francis

ONTARIO

Sorel

St. Francis River
(Alsigôntikuk)

Montreal

Yamaska River

Canada

United States

Missisquoi River

Lake Memphremagog

Lake Champlain
(Petonbowk)

Lamoille River

Winooski
River

VERMONT

MAINE

NEW YORK

Crown
Point

Otter Creek

White River

Connecticut River
(Kwanitewk)

NEW HAMPSHIRE

Lake George

Fort
Number 4

The borders to the U.S. states and Canadian provinces are current.

Saxso's Route ▬▬ ▬▬   ▬▬   ▬▬

CONTENTS

PROLOGUE

As I stood beside the river, I wondered if I had strength enough left within me. I was still weak from my wound. The smell of the burned village behind me still hung in the air, threatening to weaken my spirit.

Saxso, said a small, bitter voice within me, *you are not a man. You have been fooling yourself about that, calling yourself the head of your family. You have already failed your mother and sisters once. Why should it be different now? What can you, a boy of fourteen winters, hope to do where the best warriors have failed? Those winter people will kill you as they did the others.*

I shook my head and pushed the canoe off from the shore. I could not give in to fear or uncertainty. My family needed me.

When I was small, one of my favorite stories was of the winter people. It filled me with such excitement and dread that I could hardly bear to listen. My legs trembled while it was being told. For days after, I would wake in the night, certain that cold, sharp claws were touching me in the dark or that something thirsty for my blood was lurking in the shadows. I did not cry out. I had been taught as a very small child that crying out in the night might tell an enemy where you were. But I would listen carefully, my heart pounding in my chest, afraid that this time was not just a dream.

How does that story go? Not long ago, my mother would say—telling me this tale was not from the ancient times, but still going on among us—there was a man who was filled with greed. He was tall and gaunt. He lived alone at the edge of the village. This man did not share anything with the people. Although he was very good at hunting animals and catching fish, he never shared what he caught. He kept it all for himself. Yet no matter how much he ate, he was always hungry and he never became fat. His body got thinner and thinner. All that grew was the hunger within him. So he began to steal food from the other people in the village, eating it at night in the secrecy of his wigwam. One night, he was caught stealing food from the wigwam of an old man and woman too weak to get food for themselves. The people were shocked. How could anyone be so greedy as to steal from sick elders? They banished that man, sending him into the forest.

It was the time of year when the days grow short. Darkness came, snow began to fall. As that greedy man wandered through the forest, he did not think of the bad things he had done. All he thought of was the pain of hunger in his belly. He howled like a lone wolf driven from its pack, and the winter wind answered his howl. The winter wind came to him. It blew through him, freezing the small bit of human warmth remaining in his heart. He forgot that he was ever human. His hunger grew even greater, gnawing at his belly the way mice chew the dry bones of a deer. As he wandered, his clothing fell away in tatters. His fingernails turned into claws and his teeth grew long and sharp like those of the wildcat. Hair grew to cover his body. His hunger became so great that he tore at the flesh of his own arms. He ate away his lips. Blood dripped from his mouth. Yet nothing ever satisfied his hunger. Like others before him, that greedy man had become a Kiwakwe, one of the winter people, one of those whose heart is ice.

"That one is there in the forest to this day," my mother would say. "He never comes too close to our little village, except at night. You sometimes hear his howl on the storm wind. When you hear that terrible cry, you must run away from it as quickly as you can. Find the safety of your lodge, where the heat of the fire may keep him away. For when he hunts now, he hunts human beings. Around his neck, he wears a necklace of human skulls."

So my gentle mother would tell the story, reminding me to always be warm-hearted and generous, urging me to be careful and remain aware when I was alone in the forest. Little did I know that one night I would find another meaning for the tale. Our whole village would hear the awful howls of those hungry for our blood. On that night, even the safety of our lodges would not be enough.

1

THE BUSH THAT TALKED

I will start my story with that night. Father Roubaud used to laugh when I tried to tell a story. "Saxso," he would say, "you take too long getting into it." If I was trying to tell about a hawk catching a rabbit, he concluded, I would begin when that hawk's grandmother was still an egg.

I will try not to do that. I will jump right into the middle now, the way some of us leaped into the river to flee the Bostoniak guns. I shall begin with the whispering Mahican. His soft whisper was the first sound I heard that night. Small as it was, it broke the peace of St. Francis, our little Abenaki Indian mission village on the bank of Alsigonitikuk, the St. Francis River.

That whisper. It raises the hair on the back of my neck each time it creeps into my memory like a spider crossing your face as you sleep. It troubles me even more than the popping of the Long Knife guns that came before dawn, shattering the night.

I was standing outside the dance hall when I heard it. I had just looked around to be sure no one else was in sight. The only person who had been outside was Little Azonis Msadokwes. She had brushed past me without speaking, a strange look upon her face as she hurried back into the dance hall. I almost spoke to her. She shoved by so heedlessly that she elbowed me hard in the side. That was no way for someone an entire two winters younger than me to act.

It was the sort of thing my little sister Katrin would do. Just that morning she had spoken to me improperly after I told her—quite rightly—that she needed to be more helpful around the house.

"You never play anymore," she had said, scowling and thrusting her lips out at me. "Even your friends Piel and Antoine have noticed this. All you do is act stern."

Katrin refused to show me proper respect even after my mother urged her to listen to me. (Though perhaps it would have been better had my mother not turned her head away as if to hide a smile as she spoke.)

I considered following Little Azonis to ask why she had been so rude. She should not treat someone who was the dignified head of his family that way. Then I thought better of it. I had been drinking a lot of cider—so much that I had forgotten to act proper and grown up. I had, in fact, been laughing rather foolishly with Piel and Antoine. For some reason, my antics had made my mother nod her head at me, as if she was glad that I was forgetting my role as the responsible man of the family.

Finally, I had drank so much that I had no choice but to go outside. I stepped off the porch, unbuttoned, relaxed, and then . . .

"Ndapsi!"

The hissed word came from the bush in front of me.

Strange, I thought. *Why would a bush call me a friend? And why would it speak Abenaki with a Mahican accent?*

"My friend," the bush whispered again. Its voice sounded strained—perhaps because it was a rosebush, a very thorny one. It was so thorny that my mother said she was sure it had to be an English rosebush. My mother had brought two of those bushes from Montreal. One she planted by our house. The other, the larger of the two, she placed there by the Council Hall, the largest building in our town, where we always held our dances. Such a fine bush had to be placed where all the people could see and enjoy it. It smelled like the perfume Mother loved to get from the French. She had traded four deerskins for two rosebushes.

It was a very good trade, I now realize. Though it was trampled by the booted feet of many Bostoniak as they tried to dislodge our few stubborn defenders from the Council Hall, the rosebush grew up again from its roots. It still blooms each summer—red as the spilled blood of our people.

Whoever is in that bush will be in trouble with my mother, I thought. *My mother is proud of that bush and will not be happy if its branches are broken.* In fact, I thought I, too, would be in trouble with her if she had seen me relieving myself into it only the moment before the whisper came.

From the uncomfortable rustling sound, it seemed as if the rose was holding its own. It was a stubborn rosebush. Though it was late autumn, the bush still clung to a few dried blossoms and most of its leaves.

"*Nidoba,*" the voice whispered yet again, "if you hear me, say yes with your hand."

I held out my right hand and moved my index finger up and down. I was outlined by the light from the doorway behind me and knew that my small gesture would be seen.

"*Kedodemokawleba.* I must warn you. It is the Long Knives," said the whisperer. "They are here. All around the village to the north and east and south. *Kedatsowi wakwatahogaba!* They will wipe you out! Some of them watch your Council Hall even now. Tell the people they must get the elderly, the women, and children away. Get them away from the village. They aren't safe here."

"Samadagwis?" I said. "Is that you?"

What seemed to be a sob, a very small one, came from the shadowed shape that I was now beginning to make out crouched low in the bushes.

"I am no one," said the voice I had indeed recognized, even though four winters had passed. It was the voice of Samadagwis, the Skaticook Indian man who had once lived in our village, as had many others of his nation. He had planned to marry my cousin Beatrice. When she died of a fever, he had gone back to the south. A few of his people still remained below Fort Orange where the English had claimed the land. We had heard that he was living among the Stockbridges. They are the Indians who often served as scouts for the White Devil Rogers and his Rangers. The Stockbridges hated our allies the French. The Stockbridges would have been happy to help the Bostoniak attack us.

My mind leaped ahead like a salmon jumping frantically over the stones and waterfalls of a river in spring flood. I could already hear the guns and the screams, I could already feel the flames and smell the burning houses. I could see our stone church falling in upon itself with an awful roar.

I knew there was no time. I had to warn our people. I had to look to the safety of my mother and sisters. But I had to ask.

"Kegwi?" I said. "Why?"

No answer came.

2

THE BOSTONIAK

Why? Possible reasons raced through my mind. It began in the time of our struggles with the Bostoniak. In those days our family did not live at St. Francis. Like all the others in our little mission village, we came here to seek refuge.

Our old hunting grounds were in the long valley near the Beaver Tail Hill that gave my great-grandfather his name—Beaver's Tail. When Earth was still being shaped, Giant Beaver had been greedy and cut down all the trees to build a huge dam. He made it to hold all the water in the river for himself. The fish could no longer run upriver. The people suffered. So Gluskabe had come and fought the Giant Beaver. He broke open the dam to let the waters flow free. He killed the monster and turned his body into a range of hills. Where the dam had been was now a waterfall.

It was there, in Village Below the Falls, that my great-grandfather's father tried to greet and welcome the Bostoniak.

"They came to us because they were greedy for the furs of the animals in our forests," Beaver's Tail once told me. Though stooped with the weight of so many seasons, he was still half a head taller than any other man in our village. People say that my own tall frame is like that of my great-grandfather's. He no longer is among us, having walked the road of stars seven winters ago when I was in my own seventh year, but he lived to an old, old age.

I remember how the long fingers of his hands curled in upon themselves like two pieces of rawhide left out in the sun and rain. He could no longer use a bow or a gun, but was able to carve with a crooked knife. I can still see the strong easy motions of his hands as he worked on that soft piece of basswood while talking. Small shavings curled off the wood with each word. Though his hands shook, the knife never seemed to make a mistake and he never cut himself.

He held up the knife to let the firelight glint off its curved blade. "You sharpened this well, grandson," he said. It made me smile. It was an honor to be trusted with his favorite bone-handled blade. I wanted to be trusted. It was as important to me then as it is now, though I did not know then how badly I would fail my family during that night of blood and many guns.

"When the Bostoniak came," Beaver's Tail told me, "we thought it might be a good thing. We have always traded with other people. It was so in the days when our knives were made of flint. The best flint came from the Mohawks on the other side of the Waters Between. Though we sometimes fought, trade wove us together the way different-colored strips of basswood become a basket. The best thing carried by that basket of trade was peace. We would meet the Mohawks with our weapons held out in front of us. We would exchange weapons as a sign of respect."

My great-grandfather sighed. "So, when my father and uncle first met those men from Boston, they held out their bows in front of them. They had done the same with the French, who understood. The French had accepted our gift in a respectful way, gave us muskets, and then grasped our hands. But the Bostoniak grabbed those bows and threw them on the ground. Then they pushed my father and uncle down onto the ground and kicked them. They thought my father and uncle were cowards surrendering their weapons."

My great-grandfather paused again and turned his face toward the summer land. He was seeing that scene again as he looked toward the place where we had once lived.

"The Bostoniak," he said, returning again to his carving, "wanted the land that we lived on. They wanted us to either leave our land or be buried beneath it. We tried to make peace. When there was no other way, we fought."

This time when he paused, it was for a long time. "Village Below the Falls was a beautiful, peaceful place," Beaver's Tail said. "Many tribes came there. No one fought at the place where we fished. War in that blessed spot was unthinkable. The children played in the pools of water while their mothers smoked the fish on racks near the edge of the stream. That morning the men left to go hunting, and although I was only a boy, I went with them. We would not be gone long. I did not even think to look back and wave at my mother."

My great-grandfather sighed and looked again toward the south with clouded eyes. "We found them when we returned from hunting," he said. "All our loved ones had been slaughtered. Mothers and sisters, wives and little ones. We realized then that the hearts of the Bostoniak were filled with winter. They did not make war in the way of real human beings. They fought with no honor."

Great-Grandfather Beaver's Tail stopped speaking then, even though his hands continued their work, the shape that he was carving still hidden by his big hand. I looked up into his face. There were tears in his eyes.

He opened his hand and I saw what he had been making. It was small, but easy to recognize. It was a Kiwakwe, the winter monster that had once been a human being before greed froze its heart.

When my friend Mrs. Susannah Johnson lived among us as a captive, she taught me English. She lived in the house of Chief Gill for more than two years, so I received many such lessons.

"I have been to Boston. Have you been to Boston?" she would ask.

"*Non*," I would say. "I 'ave not been dere."

"*No, I *have* not been *there*," she would say slowly, and then I would try to speak that way.

One autumn day, I went to see her to get a shirt she had sewn for my father. He had given me a shilling to pay her for her good work. It was a fine white shirt, and my father had liked it very much. A year later he was buried wearing that shirt.

Before I left that day, I asked Mrs. Johnson a question. "Have you been to our old place by the falls?" I asked.

"What place, Saxso?" she said.

I led her there with my words, just as my great-grandfather had done for me when I was small, by describing the route a person would take to walk from St. Francis.

Mrs. Johnson smiled. "I have been there," she said. "It is named Turner's Falls. The people who live there are very proud of their town."

"Does the water still run red below the falls?" I asked. The pain and the anger I felt at that moment surprised me as much as they did my friend Mrs. Johnson. From the look that came slowly over her face, I saw that she understood. She, too, had been told about what happened there in 1676. But having lived among us for five seasons, she no longer saw it just as a great victory for the Bostoniak.

The massacre of our people at Turner's Falls was the beginning of our first war with the English. For more than eighty winters we have been at war with them. There have been times of truce, good years when we have taken our beaver skins to the truck masters at the trading posts in their forts and brought back their goods to our families. But each time, the peace has been broken by the Bostoniak. Then we have fought back. Their villages, too, have burned. Deerfield was destroyed and the Bostoniak retreated south. But they returned. So, with the French urging us on, we have continued to strike at their villages.

The French were our friends even before we went to war against the Bostoniak. When the epidemics burned through our villages like wildfires and our old medicines were of no help, Frenchmen came among us to tend the sick. They learned our language and sought to win us to their Sazos Klist, the son of the Great Spirit. Some of them seemed to love our people even more than their own. So we decided to fight by their side when the French went to war against the English.

When we left our homelands and retreated north, to Missisquoi and here to St. Francis, the French aided us. They brought us churches and priests, helped us build new homes. They gave us their Jesuit rings, like this one I wear upon my left hand. Whenever I am nervous, the fingers of my right hand seek that ring to trace the letters upon it again and again: IHS . . . IHS . . . IHS . . . IHS.

The French, though, were too few. There were a thousand English for every Frenchman. That is why we took so many young captives from the English towns. Our French brothers paid us well for such captives, and we needed the money since the beaver had grown scarce and game animals were fewer. The French believed that young people, even young Bostoniak, could still be taught to live honorably. The French used the great teachings of Sazos Klist to melt their English hearts. They made those young men and women into good French people, adding to their numbers.

The English think we are bloodthirsty savages. I have heard this from the mouths of white captives surprised at how well we treated them. They did not expect us to honor their women, to show tenderness to their children. They expected us to act like beings with hearts of ice. They thought to see hundreds of white scalps hanging in our wigwams as we danced about the fire like the monsters in their nightmares. They had not expected houses of log and stone, or that we would dress much as they dressed and that our best dances would be not of war but of thanksgiving and friendship.

When they truly saw who we were and how our lives were lived, the hearts of some of those white captives melted. A few even chose to remain with us, learn our language and become real human beings. Perhaps, even more than our raids, that was what made us most dangerous in the eyes of the Bostoniak.

I understood why the whispered words of that hidden Mahican were true. I knew why the Bostoniak and their Indian scouts were out there in the night. I knew what bloody deed they planned. They planned to kill us all.

3

THE WORRIER'S WARNING

All those thoughts rushed through my head as quickly as a deer fleeing from a hunter. No more than a heartbeat had passed since I had spoken that one word: *Kegwi*. Why? No answer was returned to me, but I knew the warning was real.

I quickly turned to go back into the Council Hall. I needed to find my mother and sisters; it was my responsibility to protect them. I knew they would still be together, just as I had left them. Even before my father's death, my sisters had always been close by my mother's side. But in this last year it had been as if the three were tied together by a cord. That was especially true of Katrin, who was only eight. Though she stubbornly believed that she knew more than anyone else, she could always be found leaning against my mother.

Marie-Jeanne, though, had begun to stretch that cord. She was now almost as beautiful as my mother, and in her own quiet way Marie-Jeanne was aware of her beauty. At the age of eleven, her thoughts had turned to such things as how her hair and clothing looked. She had begun to think of other things as well: When I had stepped outside, Marie-Jeanne had been standing as close as possible to Antoine Gill. She had been waiting for the dance that would call for people to take the hands of those next to them.

Marie-Jeanne had already decided that Antoine was the one she would marry. But he himself didn't know it yet. Since Antoine was one of my two best friends, I had been faced with the problem of telling him my sister's intentions—and thus betraying her—or allowing her to make her plans without his knowing about them. When I had asked my mother for advice, she had just smiled.

"But should I not warn Antoine?" I said. "Should he not at least know that Marie-Jeanne is already deciding what sort of dress she will wear at their wedding?"

"Saxso," my patient mother answered, "it does not matter if Antoine knows or doesn't know. It is not up to you to speak."

Now, though, was very different. It *was* up to me to speak.

The music was still going on. The sound of the rattles and the frame drums filled my ears. The sound of singing voices and stomping feet surrounded me like an embrace. People were weaving about the room, their hands linked together in the friendship dance.

Wi gai wa neh
Wi gai wa neh
This is such fun
This is such fun

There was so much to celebrate that evening. It was just before the first frost, and we had brought in the remains of the harvest. Our store of squash and corn and beans was enough to last the two hundred people of St. Francis through the hard winter. Though it was a warm evening and many, like myself, had stepped outside to cool themselves, we knew that winter was coming all too soon, and that we would be ready. We were celebrating a good hunt as well. Several deer were hanging near the smokehouse where their meat would be cured. Also, a wedding had just taken place in the church. *Truly,* I thought as I went back in, *every mind in St. Francis except mine is free of care this night.*

I quickly corrected myself. The Worrier was not free of care. Nor was he here taking part in this dance. The Worrier was the last of our *medawlinnoak,* those who see beyond the visible world in which we live. The Worrier was not his real name, but the nickname everyone called him. He had no French name, no baptismal name. He had never accepted Sazos. Strangely, he and our priest were great friends. I cannot bring the Worrier to my mind without seeing Father Roubaud engaged in discussion with him. The Worrier was a short man, one of those jokingly described as walking in a trench, while Father Roubaud was tall and thin. Seeing them argue was like watching a wood-chuck and a heron debate.

"I am worried for your soul," Father Roubaud would say in Abenaki, making a joke about the Worrier's nickname. That would bring a smile to the old man's face.

"I, too, am worried for my soul," the Worrier would reply. "I am worried that if it goes to the heaven of your Sazos Klist, there will be no one else there but Frenchmen."

Then the two of them would laugh together.

Often our people listened to the Worrier. Our hunters, in particular, paid close attention. He was always right when he told them where to find game animals, although he never failed to express concern that they would forget to show the proper respect to those animals. He knew best when the frost had passed and it was safe to put in our crops. Of course, he always feared that some hasty people would plant too soon. His constant worries about every-thing usually made us smile. But during the last few days, the Worrier had been intolerable.

"I fear that our village will be destroyed," he kept saying.

He had begun seven dawns ago, the day before the run-ner from Missisquoi told us about the hidden boats. "Our village will be destroyed, our village will be destroyed." That was all he said to anyone from the time he came into St. Francis at sunrise to the time he left at twilight.

Finally, Chief Joseph-Louis Gill could stand it no longer. He and a few others went to the Worrier's wigwam, near the edge of the ravine two and a half miles up the river from St. Francis. I was not one of those chosen by Chief

Gill to come with him. However, I followed behind the small group of men. No one told me that I could not come along. Chief Gill did turn back and scowl at me, but I simply nodded to him and smiled. How can the young learn the right way to behave unless they watch their elders?

I had always liked the Worrier. I felt bad that so many were now saying the old man had finally lost his mind. True, there were enemies abroad, they said, but that was often so. The Bostoniak Rangers who left their canoes near Missisquoi were not looking for St. Francis. They were on their way to join Wolfe and his army at Quebec. That was why the French had sent almost every available man to defend Quebec against the Englishmen.

The French had even taken many of our best fighters; they had set out three dawns ago to intercept those Bostoniak rangers. Thirty of our men were in the two militia detachments searching for enemies at the mouth of Alsigontikuk and seven miles away near Yamaska.

It was while scouting for such a party that my father had been killed a year ago in the Moon When the Leaves Fall. Surely those French soldiers and our men would find the Rangers and defeat them now as they had done near Fort Carillion in the battle on snowshoes. And if any Rangers should escape, they would have an unpleasant surprise waiting for them. Our cousins at Missisquoi had found and taken their hidden canoes and provisions.

When we reached the Worrier's wigwam, the old man was sitting calmly in front of it—as if he had been waiting for our group to arrive.

"Grandfather," Chief Gill said, "you are frightening some of the people and boring the others. Is there nothing else you can say?"

The Worrier looked up at the men who stood before him, his eyes seeking their faces one by one. I was standing back from the others, trying not to be noticed, but the Worrier turned his face toward me as well. As he did so, it seemed that his eyes grew warmer for a moment. He gave me an almost imperceptible nod. Then he looked back up at Chief Gill.

"Grandson," the Worrier said in a slow voice, "I am glad that you have finally recognized me as your grandfather."

The way he said it made Gabriel Annance, who stood to Chief Gill's left, laugh out loud. Chief Gill's face reddened. As everyone knows, despite the fact that his wife is Indian by birth and the grandniece of the Worrier, Joseph-Louis Gill's father and mother were both white captives who lived out their lives with us after being adopted by our people. Chief Gill's hair is blonde and his skin so fair that when he blushes, it is like watching the clouds change color at the approach of dawn. Yet even though his blood is white, no one doubts that Chief Gill's heart is Abenaki. When he signs his name upon documents, it is not with Joseph-Louis Gill but with his Abenaki name: Magwawidobait, "Comrade of the Mohawks."

There was a long silence as the Worrier looked up at the

four men and they looked back at him, waiting. Despite the fact that a cold wind was blowing that day, the small old man wore nothing more than a deerskin loincloth. You could see the tattoos on his chest, the designs of open-winged birds, stars, and signs of the four directions. Circling all the way around his body was the shape of the big snake that lives in the pond at the southern edge of our village and only comes out at night to speak to the *medawlinno*.

The rest of us were fully dressed. Our clothing was a mixture of the old and the new. Chief Gill wore a coat of deerskin and wampum over a finely embroidered shirt made of French cloth. My own shirt was much like his, but I wore a loincloth and leggings rather than trousers. Though Chief Gill and I had on moccasins, the two other men wore boots with soles upon them. So it is that our people adopt practical things without discarding older ways. But not the Worrier. He never wore anything that even looked as if it came from the Awanigeekneegeek, the white people.

Finally, the old man tapped his chest. "I have seen it," he said. "It was first told to me in a dream. Then, seven days ago, the Forest Dweller, the old one who watches over our village, came to me. He made signs to me that we must leave."

The Worrier paused, letting the silence deepen again.

My mind was racing. Had he truly seen the Forest Dweller, the one who looks like a giant human being but is as hairy as a bear, the one who never speaks? Like us, he once lived in the lands to the south, but followed us here to the north, allowing himself to be seen now and then so the people would know he was still with us.

The Worrier sighed. "You will not listen. Have you not noticed that I did not come into the village this morning?"

Chief Gill and the others exchanged looks. It was true. It was well after dawn, yet the Worrier was sitting here in front of his own wigwam. He was not in St. Francis, walking from house to house, striking the stone walls, the bark shingles, the planks of each building in turn, and crying out in a mournful voice, "Our village will be destroyed."

"Now I can only wait," the Worrier said. "I have seen it. I have felt the heat of the fires. Your house," he said, looking at Gabriel Annance, "and yours, Mohawk Lover. They will be nothing but ashes. Sumacs will grow up where once our village stood."

From downriver we heard the sound of the church bell ringing. It was nine o'clock. Father Roubaud was calling the children of St. Francis in for catechism lessons.

The Worrier shook his head. "It saddens me to think that soon I will never hear that bell ring again."

4

IN THE DANCE HALL

The warmth from the fire washed over me as I stood at the edge of the large room where the festivities were taking place. Not too long ago, such a celebration would have been held within a bark longhouse. Our big Council Hall, though, was not made of bent saplings lashed together. It was large enough to hold everyone in St. Francis. Like many of the homes in our village, it was a building of squared timbers with a wood floor and a stone foundation, similar to those in Montreal or Three Rivers.

In fact, our houses looked much like those used by our friends the French. And by the Bostoniak as well. Mrs. Johnson had told me of the great surprise she felt when she saw our mission village for the first time, its sixty or so neatly built houses arranged in a horseshoe with the steeple of the church rising up from among them. There were log cabins and homes made of squared timbers covered with boards. There were also four houses made of stone.

"I thought for a moment that I had been brought back to a town of my own people," she had said. "It was so far from what I had expected that if anyone had told me about it when I was back in Charlestown, I would surely not have believed it."

The only person who lived in a bark wigwam was, as I have already told you, the Worrier. However, it was not uncommon for our men and women to still make small wigwams as hunting camps when far away from St. Francis. As a child, like most of the other boys and girls, I had often made my own little wigwam in the woods north of the village and spent many a happy hour there when I should have been helping my parents or praying in the church. Little did we know that all too soon we would no longer be able to enjoy our fine houses or hear the voice of a French priest speaking the mass in Latin.

People were now joining their voices in another of our songs of celebration and friendship. The strong rhythm of single-headed frame drums, held by their rawhide strings and struck by a stick held in the right hand, throbbed like the heartbeat of our village. My friend Piel played a hand drum, while his sister shook a rattle drum fastened to the end of a stick. There were many other drums and rattles being struck or shaken together in such a way that it was as if the song held the breath of all our people.

I found myself looking so intently at the people, at their

faces, at the motions of their hands and feet, that for a moment I felt unable to move. I could hardly take a breath. I looked at the drums and rattles, at the planks of the floor beneath my feet. It was as if I was beginning to rise up out of my body, and I could hear the pounding of my own heart in my ears louder than the sounds of our music. Everything began to spin about me and I started to fall forward.

Two strong arms grabbed me. *"Saxso, nidoba! Yo kagwi? Kagwi yo?"*

It was Piel. He had seen the look upon my face, seen me start to stumble. Before I could fall, he had stopped playing his drum and stepped forward to grab hold of me.

"I . . . I am all right," I said. "But something is going to happen, a terrible thing."

Piel pointed with his lips across the room. "That is what she says also," he said.

I looked. There was a small knot of people gathered around someone who was talking with great earnestness and making gestures. It was Azonis Msadokwes. I understood now why she had brushed past me as I made my way outside, why that look had been upon her face. I knew that my own face now wore that same look of shock and near disbelief. She, too, had heard a whispered warning from Samadagwis. People were listening closely to her, but some were shaking their heads.

I moved nearer. The drumming and dancing had stopped. Many were listening to what the man in front of Azonis was saying, though some turned in my direction as I approached. I was told later that my face was like that of one who has seen *jibayodep*, the head of a ghost, floating toward him out of the mist.

"She is only a child," someone was saying. "She has imagined it."

I looked at the man who was talking. It was Nanagonsikon. Though he was an elder, he was not as well-respected as most of the men of his age. Perhaps it was because he was always disagreeing with everyone. "It is too bad," my father had said to me once, "that old Nanagonsikon did not take his own advice and go off to join the western Indians as he wanted the rest of us to do."

I found myself wishing, as I did so often, that my father was still among us and not walking the road of stars. I wished that my uncle Pierre and the other men of our village had not joined the French soldiers to search for the enemy Bostoniak. It was not just that they had taken most of our guns. It was also that they knew how to fight. Few left in our village that night had as much experience of war or were as good with a musket. Captain Panadis had gone off to Quebec to hunt game for the French soldiers. Chief Gill and his closest companions were also away hunting deer, though their wives and children were here at the dance.

Nanagonsikon laughed in an unpleasant way. "She has heard too many stories, this girl child."

"*Nda,*" I said. "*Non.*"

The loudness of my voice surprised me. Every eye in the dance hall was now turned in my direction, including those of my highly critical little sister Katrin. *I am a child too,* I thought. *Will they listen to me?*

Old Nanagonsikon stared at me as if I was a piece of meat that had gone bad, but others were clearly waiting to hear what I had to say. Best of all, I could see my mother's face now. She nodded her head, and her look was one of complete trust. Next to her, my sister Marie-Jeanne was mouthing a word as she lightly held my mother's right hand: *Geloziidokan*. Speak, elder brother. Knowing that my family believed in me gave me strength. I ignored for the moment the fact that Katrin was making a rude face at me as she peered out from behind my mother's skirt.

I took a deep breath. "Azonis is speaking the truth. There are enemies around the village."

"How do you know?" a woman asked from behind me. I knew from the strength of her soft, clear voice who it was. It was Chief Gill's wife, Marie-Jeanne, my sister's namesake. Her father had also been a chief, and many felt that she was the true power behind her husband's chieftaincy. It was certain that she was always his first and best advisor.

"There was a Mahican hidden in the bushes. He was among the Stockbridge scouts leading a war party of Bostoniak Rangers. But he slipped away to warn us because he knows this village. It was Samadagwis."

I heard people draw in breath.

"That is how the blind Englishmen found our village," said someone in the crowd of people around me. "They never could have done it without other Indians betraying us."

It was Gabriel Annance. He had planned to go hunting with Chief Gill but stayed behind because his stomach was bothering him. Most felt, though, that his stomach ailment was just an excuse to keep him from missing the dance. Everyone knew Gabriel had eyes for Marie-Appoline Gill, Chief Gill's lovely sister. Indeed, Gabriel's bad stomach had not kept him from dancing near her the entire night, leaning close to engage in laughing conversation whenever there was a pause in the singing.

"Jah," the red-faced man standing next to Gabriel Annance said. "Dose Stockbridge! Ve never should have let dem visit St. Francis." It was Jahn Hennesse, a German who had been taken captive by one of our raiding parties. He had married Chief Gill's sister Jeanne-Magdeleine twenty-five years ago. Even though he spoke our language with a strange accent, he now considered himself more Abenaki than many of our people with no European blood at all. His son, Jean—who many said would one day become a chief— was one of those who had gone off with that French party to try to find the enemy.

Others began to speak up. Not everyone believed the warning. Some agreed with old Nanagonsikon that there was no danger. But the majority of the people felt just the opposite. They remembered what had happened at Norridgewock in August of 1724. The English had surrounded that village in the Kennebec Valley. More than 120 people had been killed, the town burned. No mercy had been shown to women and children. The survivors who fled north had told us how even the church was destroyed. Father Rasles, their priest, had been killed too. Most of those Norridgewocks went back to the Kennebec, but the stories of the massacre remained with us. Mothers sometimes frightened their children into obedience by telling them that the Bostoniak, led by the White Devil Rogers, would come and eat them if they did not behave.

Some of our men proposed to barricade themselves in the Council Hall and wait for the enemies. "No one will drive us from our village," François Loron said. Then, without another word to anyone, he slipped out the door of the dance hall to get his musket from his house. A handful of other men left to do the same, determined to make a fight of it here or from their homes.

Others began to make different plans. There were several ways out of the village. If people could reach the ravine or the pines, they might be safe there. Though it was uncertain where the enemies now were or how many of them were around us, it was unlikely they would attack from either of those directions.

Father Roubaud was not in St. Francis that night. He had no great opposition to our dances, but liked to go to bed early. Since there was little possibility anyone could sleep while the singing and dancing was going on, our priest had chosen to absent himself, traveling to visit another missionary. When he returned the next day, would anything be left for him to return to?

Several women, the most determined of Father Roubaud's followers, decided to seek refuge in the church. "Sazos Klist will protect us in his holy place," they said.

The people who seemed most afraid were those who had once been English. Though their skin was still white, they no longer thought themselves Bostoniak. More than death, they feared being taken by force back to the heartless towns of the Bostoniak to the south. The women would once again be the property of husbands and fathers, no longer able to make their own decisions. Both men and women who had learned to live and speak as Indians would be treated with contempt. There was a lost look upon the paler faces of our adopted brothers and sisters.

The music had stopped. Everyone was talking at once. Aside from the men who had gone to collect their weapons and the women who had headed to the church, most of the people were still inside the dance hall.

My mother and sisters were now by my side. Marie-Jeanne put her hand on my arm and smiled at me. "You spoke well," she whispered. To my surprise, Katrin grabbed my wrist with both of her hands. I looked down at her. It seemed for a moment as if she was going to say something, but she quickly let go and turned to embrace my mother's waist, hiding her face from me.

I turned to my mother. She could see my indecision. Should I stay and try to help the men who would barricade themselves in the Council Hall? The nervous fingers of my right hand sought my Jesuit ring.

My mother pointed with her chin in the direction of the door. "François and the others are brave men," she said in her soft voice. My mother never speaks loudly, but her words are so strong that one cannot help but listen. "They may be throwing their lives away," she said, "but they know it. They are playing the part of Mother Partridge when

Wonkses, the fox, comes close to her chicks. You know how she pretends her wing is broken and makes a great commotion to draw danger away from her family."

My mother placed her hand upon my shoulder. "There are enough of them to do that, Saxso. It would help us greatly if you came with us."

I nodded. Since my father was gone, it fell upon me to take his place. I must care for my mother and sisters. Though I wished I could stay and try to fight the men who would soon attack our village, it was my responsibility to stay by my family.

The sound of the drum suddenly began again. People turned to look. Antoine Gill now held one of the drums and was playing it. There was a look of great determination on his handsome face.

Piel, too, picked up a drum. "Dance," he shouted. Then he began to sing the greeting song, his voice as deep and strong as someone twice his age.

As one, the people seemed to understand. The confusion of voices debating what to do ended. Many voices joined in the song, and dancing feet again struck the wooden floor. What seemed like joyous music poured out of the windows into the night. If anyone had been listening from some place of concealment outside our village, he might think that there had only been a pause in the celebration while people rested. Now all seemed to be going on just as it had been before. But it was not so. The music being played and sung was meant to make the ears of our enemies deaf. It was not a song of welcoming, but of survival.

Small groups of people began leaving the building. Some moved toward the deep ravine or the forest. Others went to their homes. They took no lights with them. Their steps were silent and careful. There was no shouting, no crying, no headlong flight. Instead, our people moved like shadows, leaving the village the way mounds of ice leave the banks of the river, melting away so slowly that no notice might be taken until all were gone.

5

THE RAVINE

Piel and Antoine were still drumming and singing. Each of them now held a rattle in addition to their drum sticks so that it would seem as if at least four people were making the music. I looked back at my two friends and caught their eyes.

"*Wlipamkaani, nidobak,*" I mouthed. "Travel well, my friends."

They nodded back to me and continued that welcoming song, even though they knew that it might be answered all too soon not by the voices of friends but by the sharp crack of muskets.

I left the Council Hall with my mother and my two sisters. We moved as slowly and stealthily as deer trying to slip past waiting hunters, but my mind was running. Was there nothing more I could do? What would my warrior father have done? Was there no way that we could get help before the attack came?

There were so few men in St. Francis now that we could not hope to fight off these enemies. Six years of constant war had lessened our numbers. Some, like my father, had died in the forefront of battle. Others, weary of war and uncertainty, had left to settle elsewhere. Before all of that our village had numbered almost a thousand souls, as we had brought the Skaticook Mahicans in among us. Life had no longer been either good or safe for them along the Mahicanitewk near Fort Orange. So a rescue party had gone south to Albany in the fall of 1754. Everyone, except for five men who had been away hunting, had been brought to St. Francis. Those five men were forced by the Bostoniak to live among the Stockbridge and told to forget that they had ever been Mahican. Samadagwis had gone back to those few remaining relatives after the death of the woman he wanted to marry.

In my mind I quickly counted up our numbers. Perhaps fifty of our people had chosen to leave the village that night to sleep out of earshot of the drumming and singing. Some were older men who had been good fighters in their youth. They had taken their muskets with them. If they were here, they would give the Bostoniak fierce resistance. But there was no time to go and seek them out in their camping places in the woods. No more than two hundred of us were in St. Francis this night, and the majority were women and children.

If only our French allies and our warriors were closer. True, Yamaska was only seven miles away down the King's

Highway, and it would only take three hours by canoe to reach St. Francis from the mouth of our river. But much could happen in only a few hours. Our enemies were already here. Somehow they had circled around our defenders. The quiet in the woods around our village was proof of that. There were no sounds of animals or birds. Such silence only occurs when human hunters walk the night.

The people of our village were also moving silently through the darkness. A few, braver or more foolhardy than others, went toward their houses. The brave ones hoped to collect sleeping children or elders who had not been at the dance. The foolish ones planned to collect valuables and other objects dear to them.

Some, like us, turned away from the village. Our lives were dearer to us than any material possessions. We made our way toward the middle of the ravine. I was in the lead, holding tight to my sister Marie-Jeanne's hand as she followed behind me. Katrin held her hand and my mother held Katrin's, making sure that my two sisters were kept between us, linked together as if we were doing a friendship dance.

We were close behind the Obomsawin family, led by the tall figure of Simon Obomsawin. The Obomsawins had left the hall before us to collect their sleeping children. Their shapes were shadowy and indistinct in this last darkness before dawn. I had only recognized who they were when the moon briefly broke through the clouds, reflecting its light off the silver ornament that Great Simon always wore upon his black hat.

The V-shaped ravine we headed for had been cut by the small brook that runs down to the river below St. Francis. At the river itself, the mouth of the ravine is wide and very deep. Only at the top, several hundred paces from the river, is it narrow enough to step across. To reach our village our enemies would have to go around to the top of the ravine. On the village side of the ravine, halfway down to the river, a small, barely visible trail leads down through the brush and small pines. Although the big trees around the ravine had all been cut two generations ago, little pines had returned. They would help conceal us as we took the trail down into the ravine.

I squeezed Marie-Jeanne's hand. A moment later she squeezed mine back three times, a signal that all three of them were still linked together.

Simon Obomsawin stopped at the head of the trail. He was always a kind man, caring for others before himself. He waited to help us all down through the dark onto the steep, narrow path. The sky was beginning to show the signs of dawn. We had to hurry. But no one spoke above a whisper. Everyone stepped so carefully that no stones went rolling down and the fallen pine needles cushioned the sound of our feet.

When we were deep enough into the gully, our party stopped. We knew there were others hiding close by, though we could not see them. The descent had been steep, but I had never let go of Marie-Jeanne's hand.

"Mother," I whispered, reaching out my free hand into the darkness.

"I am here," she whispered back, grasping my fingers.

"And I," Katrin said in a surprisingly soft voice.

"I too," Marie-Jeanne breathed, squeezing the hand she already held. The small circle of our family was complete.

"Wligen," I said. "Good."

Though I was greatly relieved that we had all reached this place of refuge safely, I felt tense as a bowstring. Something was wrong here in the ravine. I could feel it.

"Wait here," I whispered to my mother and sisters. I crawled over toward the Obomsawin family.

"Where is she?" someone was asking in a soft, urgent voice.

"She is not here," another voice whispered.

I placed my hand on Simon Obomsawin's arm. *"Awani?* What is wrong?"

"Little Malian," Great Simon answered. His low voice was grave. "Our youngest daughter, she is not among us. We have left her at the house. I must go back for her."

My family was safe now, but I felt as if I had not done enough, not as much as my father would have done. This would be my chance. "I will go with you," I said, making my decision without another moment's thought.

Simon leaned his head close to mine. *"Tsigapi,"* he whispered. "Be silent."

I nodded my head without speaking. And then, to my everlasting regret, I followed him out of the ravine instead of going back to my mother and sisters. *They are safe,* I thought. *I have man's work to do.* I realize now that what I did was not what my father would have done. My actions were those of a foolish child.

6

MALIAN'S SONG

Great Simon placed his hand on my shoulder. We crouched low as we crossed the open land between the ravine and the edge of the village, keeping our eyes down. Several times we heard sounds that could only have been made by men concealed in the brush to the east of the village. One of those sounds was a cough, the other was something that would have made me laugh had there not been such danger.

At the village edge, we stopped and listened hard. Had we heard the sound of feet following us? We waited, but we could not wait for long. Hearing nothing further, we continued on our way. Now we were almost to his house, across the square from the Council Hall and the church.

Silence trembled around us, a seeming calm that was far

from truly peaceful. It was the last hour before dawn. No longer was there music coming from the Council Hall, but the building was not empty. I did not know how many, but men of St. Francis were waiting inside, their few muskets ready to fire at any attackers. I wondered if my brave friends Piel and Antoine were among them. In other houses around the square a handful of other men were prepared to do the same as those in the Council Hall. Concealed in the cellars and the attics of some houses were people too stubborn, too uncertain, or too old to flee. Then there were the faithful women inside the church. How many souls remained in St. Francis? Probably no more than thirty or forty people, all holding their breath to keep that tense silence. And in the stillness, I began to hear the pounding of my own heart. There was a tightness in my throat and chest.

But as we edged closer to Great Simon's house, we realized that it was not completely silent around us. We could hear the voice of a child singing softly. I shall never forget that song. I suspect that it will live long after my life and words have been forgotten. There was so much quiet courage in that song, so much knowledge for one so young.

> *Nziwaldam, nziwaldam.*
> *Anahkwihka ndodana.*
> *Malian pihta nziwaldam.*
> *Nda tomo widomba.*
>
> I am lonesome, I am lonesome.
> Our village grows up with trees.

Malian is very lonesome.
There is no friend anywhere.

It was the voice of Great Simon's little girl Malian, who had been left behind in the darkness and confusion of our flight. As we came around the side of the house, I saw her there. She sat on the end of her bed close to the open window, singing as she leaned on the sill.

I paused, entranced by her song, by the fact that this brave child did not weep or run into the night calling for help in a way that would bring the enemy down upon us. Instead she waited, singing this song that seemed to have sprung not only from her heart but from the heart of our whole village. It was a song of courage and also a song of the mourning time yet to come.

Great Simon tapped my shoulder, motioning for me to stand guard as he went inside the house. I watched as Great Simon's tall shape appeared behind his little daughter. I saw the smile that came on her face when she turned to him. I knew that the relief throbbing within her must have made her want to laugh or shout with joy, but a wisdom beyond her years told her to keep that lifesaving silence. All that she did was open her small arms for the embrace that lifted her up from the ground. Within only a few heartbeats Great Simon was outside, Little Malian held firmly in the crook of his left arm, her face pressed into his neck.

He did not speak to me. There was no need. I followed close behind as we made our way across the open ground.

But as swiftly as we moved, it was not swift enough. The attack began just as we reached the head of the path into the ravine. The crack of a musket sounded from behind us, followed by a howling that was louder than the ice-hearted spirits who prowl the forests for human prey.

7

THE ATTACK

They came into town from three directions, striking from the north, the east, and the south, seeking to catch our people in their homes or drive them toward the river, where they could be killed trying to cross. I didn't know it then. It is only now, looking back on it in my memory, that I realize what was their plan.

I did not see our enemies clearly at first. The light before dawn was only enough to make out the shapes of moving figures, sinister as the shadows of monsters from a wintertime story. From their howling war cries and the cracking of their muskets, filling the air like the sound of pine trees exploding in a forest fire, it seemed there were thousands of them. Yet there were no more than one hundred fifty Bostoniak Rangers led by Major Robert Rogers, the White

Devil, and his Stockbridge Indian scouts who had showed them the hidden ways to our village.

By now Great Simon and I had slid down onto our bellies in the brush. Little Malian, still clinging to him, made not a sound, though she turned her head to look. Her eyes were wide at what was happening. No one noticed us in our place of concealment.

A skinny man dressed in leather loped past us. He was carrying a long gun with a great knife attached to the front of it. The torch that he held in his left hand played over his gaunt, wild-eyed face. The tops of his high moccasins were sewn in the Iroquois way, down the middle from shin to toe. He passed so close we could smell him. Unlike our Indian people, white men have no love of bathing. It was a joke among us that we could smell the Bostoniak long before we could see them, but this was no time for laughter. That white man, screaming like a devil, would kill us if he could. On he ran, toward the square of houses.

I did not see what happened. But I would be told about it by those who survived. I would hear their stories while smoke still rose from the ruins of our town. I would smell the burned flesh, see the blood upon the earth, a dropped tomahawk, the broken stock of a musket. But now, following Great Simon as he clutched his precious burden, I made my way to the safety of the ravine. I did not see my mother and sisters, but, I am shamed to say, I was not thinking of them at that moment. My heart was beating so fast that my hands trembled. All I could think of was the fight that was now beginning, and what we must do to save those who were hidden.

People gathered around us, their faces not yet visible in the last darkness before sunrise. "We cannot wait here," Great Simon said, as he handed Little Malian to her mother. "The enemies might find us. We must move down to the river."

His words were wise. The enemies had not come from the river. So they had no boats. But we did. A dozen strong Abenaki canoes were beached on the shore below us. If we could reach them, we could cross to the other side and find safety. We felt our way quickly down to the shore and found the canoes.

Great Simon stood watch as one boat after another vanished into the black of the river. He would wait until everyone else was safe before he, too, went to the other side. Little Malian was in one of the first canoes to cross, her face turned in the direction of Great Simon as if her eyes were unable to see enough of him before she disappeared into the great pool of whispering darkness that was our river.

Great Simon's canoe was the last to enter. I was with him. The sun was beginning to rise and the tops of the trees could be seen. Soon we would no longer be concealed by the veil of darkness. If the Bostoniak came down to the river, they would see us.

As we paddled, I thought of the Little Ones who live beneath the surface of our river. They love our people. When enemies come toward our village by water, the Little Ones reach up, overturn their canoes, and drown them.

"Help us across," I sang. "Little Ones, help us, give strength to my arms." Our canoe seemed to move even more swiftly with my song. We had almost reached the other side.

Harsh voices were shouting from behind us. The sun had not yet struck the riverbank on our side. It would be hard to see us there in the shadows. That was good. The Bostoniak were great shots. Some carried rifles that were much more accurate than an ordinary musket. Such guns could easily hit a man from as far away as the other side of the river. But if we got away from the river's edge and into the trees, we would be safe from their guns.

All of the canoes of the village were now on the far side of the river. The enemies would not be able to use our own boats to pursue us.

I leaped from the front of the canoe.

"Hurry," Great Simon said. "Help the others up the bank."

He began to pull our canoe farther from the water, not wanting to take the chance that it might be carried by the current back to the other side. As he did so, he turned slightly. The first light from the rising sun struck the silver ornament on his black cap, making it gleam. It was all that the marksman on the other side needed. I saw the small puff of smoke from the other bank and heard the thud of the rifled musket ball that struck Great Simon a second before the echoing crack of the shot reached me.

Other shots began striking around me as I grasped Simon's arm and his shoulder, trying to pull him with me. His eyes met mine for a moment and then their light went out. His body became limp as a deer when an arrow has cut its breath. His spirit began its journey toward the highest mountain where the sky road begins.

Something hit me in the shoulder, turning me around. I fell hard on the gravel. The world was spinning and I could taste the bitterness of metal in my mouth. I looked back across the river. Though the other bank was distant, it seemed no farther than the length of my arm. A man with a face as hairy as that of a bear was reloading his long rifle and pointing in my direction as other men spilled down the bank. Their voices were angry, wild and raucous as a flock of crows. They were looking for some way to cross after us, but there were no boats left for them. Our river was too wide and swift for them to swim. Holding my hand against my shoulder, I crawled up the bank and disappeared from their sight into the brush.

I tried to run. My legs were unwilling. They collapsed beneath me as if they were broken sticks. I did not want to sleep, but my eyes closed.

When I woke, it was strangely quiet. I could no longer hear the sounds of gunfire, harsh shouts, people crying out in pain. But I knew that it had not all been a terrible dream. The smell of smoke from our burning village filled the air, blown across the river by the swirling wind coming now from the east. There was a terrible throbbing pain in my shoulder that suddenly grew sharper as something hard was pressed into it, cutting my flesh. I gasped and tried to sit up, but a small, strong hand pressed down on my forehead. I bit deeply into the stick that had been shoved into my mouth. The world spun and darkness washed down upon me.

When light returned, the Worrier was leaning over me. He took his hand from my forehead and pulled the stick out of my mouth. Tossing it aside, he reached down and picked up the musket ball that he had pried out of me with the small, slender-bladed knife made for just such a purpose. I looked at my shoulder. Something was pressed into my wound. It smelled of dust and felt as sticky as spiderwebs. I recognized the smell. The Worrier had been teaching me about his medicines. This one was largely made from a puffball mushroom. It would stop the bleeding and help the healing.

"You are lucky," the Worrier said. "The one who shot you did not put enough powder into his gun. The ball was moving too slowly to break your shoulder bone."

He held the musket ball closer for me to look at it. It was round and smooth, the lead barely dented from piercing my leather shirt and my flesh. He placed it in my hand. It would go into my pouch and stay with me, a talisman to keep me from ever being struck again.

I sat up. The pain I had felt was almost gone. My arm would try to stiffen, but if I kept moving it, perhaps that would not happen. There was no time to let that happen. I looked up at the sky. The sun was already two hands above the horizon. At least three hours had passed since the cowardly attack began.

"Great Simon?" I asked. I already knew the answer, but when the Worrier shook his head, I bit my lip.

The Worrier helped me to my feet. I looked around, seeing many of the familiar faces of those who had taken shelter with us in the ravine.

But some were missing.

I looked down at the Worrier. He answered the question that filled my mind before I had the chance to speak it.

"Your mother and sisters are not here," he said. "They did not come across the river with the others."

The pain from my wound vanished, and in its place came the feeling of a great weight within my heart. I had promised my father that I would care for them, yet when my first chance came to protect in the time of great danger, I had not stayed by them. Awful thoughts filled my mind. I saw them injured or taken captive or among the dead.

"We must go back for them," I said, my words tasting like ashes as I spoke them. "Now."

8

THE BURNED VILLAGE

As the Worrier and I recrossed the river, a large bird flew up from the reeds on the other side. Its white-banded wings were wide, and it flew straight toward us, passing over the Worrier's head as he stopped paddling to watch it. It was a loon, so close that the whistling of its wings filled my ears. For a few heartbeats its wings drowned out the crackling of the flames from the high bank where St. Francis had once stood. Then it swept past us, swift as an arrow's flight.

"*Wliwini*," the Worrier said in a soft voice as he watched the loon grow small and disappear. "Thank you, my brother, for reminding us we may rise to fly again."

As we drew closer to the riverbank, the sound of burning seemed to grow louder, though the smoke was less now. A strange roaring filled my ears. I could not feel the sand and gravel of the riverbank beneath my feet when I climbed out of the canoe. It was as if I was floating. Everything around me was unreal and yet more real than anything I had ever seen before, both at the same time.

Though the Bostoniak Rangers had thought to surprise us, they themselves had been surprised. They had not been able to kill us all in our sleep. Most of our people had escaped. It seemed that the Rangers had taken out their frustration by trying to wipe our village from the face of the earth. Almost every house had been set on fire. Those few people who had taken shelter within their attics and cellar holes were now dead. Their choice had been no choice at all: either to come out and be taken by the white men or to accept a death by smoke and flame. They would not allow these white enemies the chance to take their scalps as trophies. The price paid for an Indian scalp in Boston was a five-pound sterling note. I imagined how some of our people had screamed in pain as the choking smoke and the awful heat from the flames took their lives. Others, I knew, had died silently, not willing to give the Bostoniak the small satisfaction of hearing them cry out for help.

Our enemies did not even treat the church with respect. They attacked this house of God, breaking through the barricaded doors. They looted the silver and dragged out some of those who had taken shelter there. But they did not find everyone. When the church began to burn, the women who remained inside were trapped in the fire. The thick smoke must have carried their last prayers up to the heavens.

Only three buildings were spared, including the Council Hall, where a few of our men held out against the Rangers until they were killed or forced to retreat. The Council Hall, chosen by the White Devil himself, was then used as the rallying point for the Rangers. The other two buildings were filled with stored corn. It seems that the Bostoniak had lost most of their food supplies in their forced march to our village. They carried bags of our corn with them as they retreated. They were in great haste, for they knew the sounds of the battle could be heard from far away, the smoke seen from even farther.

Our village was gone. Even our farm animals—the cows, the pigs, the chickens—had been killed or driven off. It was as if a giant made of fire had walked through, crushing everything beneath its terrible burning feet. Only blackened timbers remained where the church, the beautiful house of Chief Gill, and dozens of other homes, including our own small cabin, had been.

Survivors had gathered in the square, seeking family and friends who had become separated during our desperate flight. I heard their anxious voices calling out.

"Piel!"

"Marie-Therese?"

"Morice?"

"My father?"

"My child!"

"My mother? My sisters?"

One of those voices crying out for lost loved ones was my own.

As I wandered about, asking for word of my family, people

told me what they had seen. Some could barely speak more than a few words without being overcome by weeping. Others, perhaps feeling as I did that they were in the midst of an incredible dream from which they would surely wake, spoke in matter-of-fact tones.

While my group had found shelter in the ravine and then crossed the river, others had hidden near Sibosek, the little brook to the north of town. Some who had gone in the wrong direction, toward the small woods upriver where the Bostoniak hid before their attack, had saved themselves by crawling into the brush and keeping quiet.

One of these was Tomas. A year younger than me, Tomas had been a white person before being adopted.

"It was like the games we played," he said, "where we would close our eyes and find each other in the woods by the sounds we made. I was sure they could not find me as long as my eyes were closed. The one time I opened them, I saw a Ranger's boot right in front of my face. But I closed my eyes before he could find me, and I heard him move away."

Tomas knelt down and began to cry. I understood his tears. I had found him standing in front of the ruins of the house where he had lived with the elderly people who had adopted him. Tamkwait and Tamakwa had been too old to run. Their bodies were somewhere beneath the charred timbers. Tamkwait and his wife were kind people. Everyone in St. Francis loved them. Tomas had once told me that he was the youngest of fourteen children. He had often been beaten. But when he misbehaved here, his new parents had just called him over to them and hugged him.

"I saw the White Devil," said a familiar voice from behind me. I turned to look into the face of François Loron. His forehead and cheeks were dark with dried blood, and his left eye was swollen shut. He was leaning on what remained of his musket. It had either burst or been struck by a ball, for the barrel was split open.

"They came into the village from three sides, howling like wolves. There were Indians with the Bostoniak. Pah!" He spat upon the ground. "Stockbridges with their faces painted white!"

Others gathered around us, listening to François's words.

"If there had been enough of us with guns, we could have killed them all. They thought to take us by surprise, kill us in our beds. Even before we began to fire at them, they were throwing their burning torches into the houses. They were fools, for their torches made them easy to see. Only their leader showed some sense. He was a big man, but not as tall as a pine, as some have said. He was ugly and his legs were skinny, but they all listened to him. He must have been Rogers, the White Devil. He was the one who had them concentrate their fire upon the Council Hall to drive us out."

Then François shook his head. "He was a better man than some of the others in his company. I saw him stop a man from thrusting a bayonet into a child. He could not be everywhere at once, but it seemed that the White Devil, at least, tried to spare the children and the women."

I looked at the Council Hall. The wood of the door and window frames was splintered all around where musket balls had struck.

"François," I said, "my mother, my sisters, did you see them?"

He looked at me. For a moment it seemed as if his eyes could see nothing but that fight, as if his mind and heart were still caught in that awful battle. Then something seemed to clear away from his gaze the way mist moves from the surface of the river.

"I am not certain," he said. "The White Devil took some of our people as captives. But I cannot say who was taken. In the smoke of the battle, I could not see for sure."

9

JEAN BAPTISTE

The Worrier grasped my arm. He had stopped to care for the wounds of a man stabbed by one of the long knives of the Rangers. I had continued on, calling out for my mother and sisters, stumbling like so many others through the confusion and pain, the smoke and the smells of blood and burned flesh.

"Come," the Worrier said. He drew me along with him toward a small group of people who were standing looking down at something. Someone. An Indian lay there just off the side of the road. For a moment I did not know him. He was so small that he looked more like an injured child than a grown person. From his clothing and the white paint on his face, I could tell he was not one of us but an enemy. He was on his back, his head resting on a hummock of sweet grass. Other clumps of the grass were around him. He had fallen in the place where we gathered the sweet grass to bring its good scent into our homes. The smell of it was all around us.

It was strange to smell it now after all the awful things that had occurred. Sweet grass was a gift from Gluskabe, the one who changed things. I had heard the story from a Penobscot man who had visited us two winters ago. Skunk, the Penobscot man said, was jealous of all the good things Gluskabe did. So Skunk walked through the grass rubbing himself on it to make it smell as bad as he did. But Gluskabe saw what Skunk had done. He breathed on that bad-smelling grass, and its scent became as sweet as his own breath. And so it was now. Despite the bitter smells of smoke and blood and death in the village close behind us, here there was that blessing scent, one that our elders told us was meant to bring health to both body and spirit.

The small enemy Indian was hurt badly. His hands were clasped over his belly to cover the great wound there. He had no weapons, neither a gun nor a war hatchet. The empty sheath that hung around his neck had once held a knife. It was unusual that he had been stripped of those things. Usually your knife is left with you when you fall in battle.

Those who were watching parted to let the Worrier and me kneel down beside him. The man groaned and tried to lift his head. It was Samadagwis.

"My friend," I said. "Your warning saved many people."

The Worrier gently moved Samadagwis's hands from the wound, then placed them back again. He felt the wounded man's legs, slid his hand around the back. I could see now that much blood had soaked into the earth beneath him, down into the roots of the sweet grass. He had been struck down away from the fighting. It was unlikely that an Abenaki had shot him. The Worrier held up four fingers. Samadagwis had been shot in the back, not once, but four times. The wound in front was where a ball had come out. The Worrier clenched both fists, placed them together, and then made a motion as if he was breaking a stick. I understood. That shot had broken the spine.

"Maguak," Samadagwis whispered. "Cowards. They knew what I had done, but they did not kill me like men. They shot from behind."

He looked up at me with calm eyes. He knew he was dying, but it did not frighten him.

"My mother and my sisters," I said. "Did you see them?"

Samadagwis breathed in slowly. One of the other shots must have broken something in his chest. The fluttering sound his breath made was like a bird beating its wings. "They are alive," he whispered. "The Bostoniak took them. I saw them."

Heavy feet thudded up.

"What is this?" an angry voice said from behind us.

It was Gabriel Annance. He was with two other Abenaki men, one of whom held a hatchet. The three angry men looked down at Samadagwis, seeing only a wounded enemy. The golden sweet grass rustled against their feet as they moved close.

Samadagwis raised a hand to push the Worrier and me

away. We did not resist. There was nothing more that we could do.

The man lifted his hatchet, ready to finish the work of death begun by the cowardly Bostoniak.

"Do not kill me yet," Samadagwis said. "I want to be baptized. I am not baptized yet."

The man with the hatchet was surprised. He lowered his weapon. "That is not good," he said. "How are you called?"

Samadagwis breathed in again, more slowly than before. There were few breaths left to him in this lifetime. When he spoke, the foam at the corners of his mouth was flecked with crimson. "I am Samadagwis," he answered.

"You have no real name?" Gabriel Annance asked. By that he meant no Christian name.

Samadagwis shook his head, though it took great effort to do it.

A memory came to me then, clear as the sound of the mission bell. Five winters ago Samadagwis had been in the house of my family. He had been standing close to Beatrice, looking up at her with a smile. She was almost a head taller than him, and was teasing him that he wanted to marry her so she could protect him. She called him My Little Mahican.

"Before we marry," he told her that day, "I will be baptized. I like your French way of praying."

The following spring the coughing sickness had taken his Beatrice from him.

"How then do you want to be called?" said the man with the hatchet, his voice softer now.

Samadagwis swallowed, trying to force the words from an unwilling throat. *"Sabadis,"* he said. "Jean Baptiste."

"To what people do you belong?" Gabriel asked, kneeling to place one hand on the wounded man's shoulder.

"Mahican," Samadagwis answered. His voice was now as thin and tight as a stretched piece of rawhide.

"That is good," said the man with the hatchet. "Now your name will be Sabadis."

So we baptize you, I thought. I turned away, the fingers of my right hand tracing the letters of my Jesuit ring. The scent of the sweet grass seemed to grow stronger around us as the hatchet was raised and brought swiftly down.

10

LITTLE PINES

There was no sense of time passing that morning. Perhaps it was because the church was gone. The church had kept the time for us with the ringing of its bell. Before the Jesuits came, we had no clocks and no word for time. Even now, when we speak of a clock, we do so with the word *papeezok-wazik,* which means "that noisy thing which does nothing useful." But that morning I longed to hear the bell ringing for the nine o'clock gathering of the faithful.

I still moved as if I was within a dream, barely aware of my feet touching the earth. Yet I kept hearing and seeing things around me with such clarity that I knew I would never forget them. Still, as in a dream, there were also things from that morning so blurred that I could not quite make them out. I remember the way a small child's hand felt when it reached up and took mine while the Worrier helped me search for my family. I never looked down at that child, separated like me from loved ones. I do not know if the little one was a boy or a girl, but I remember that we kept squeezing each other's hands. Though we spoke no words, that child and I gave each other comfort. I remember the voice of the child's mother, the touch of one of her hands on my cheek as she thanked me for helping her beloved little one. I remember their arms wrapped about each other as the Worrier and I continued on our search. But I cannot remember that woman's face, even though I know she must have been one of my neighbors, perhaps one of my own mother's best friends.

My eyes had viewed too many terrible things. Perhaps that is why I stopped seeing the burned houses, the blood, the twisted bodies, and the pained faces. My ears had heard too many awful sounds—the worst of them those whispered words that my mother and sisters were captives. Perhaps that is why after a time I became deaf to the wood crackling and popping as the fires burned themselves out. The wailing and hopeless weeping faded from my ears as we walked and walked.

It had been that way for me once before, when word came of my father's death. In the days that followed that news, my body went about doing the things that had to be done, while my soul removed itself to another place, one that such pain cannot reach. The Creator is sometimes kind to us at those times when our hearts are ready to break, giving us forgetfulness or blindness, closing our eyes or our ears to those things that would be too much for us to bear.

A noise from the sky, a sound both distant and close, brought me back to myself. I looked up to see not one but four great V's of geese. They were leaving the cold of the winter land, making their long journey back to the summer country. Their cries were like the yelping of dogs. As I heard them, my mind saw again the pitiful sight that had greeted us when the Worrier and I had reached the eastern edge of St. Francis. Our village had had many dogs. They had always roamed about together as if in their own small clan. But they would roam no longer to chase rabbits, be shouted at when they scavenged a bit of meat, or play with our children. The bodies of our dogs lay at the edge of the village where the Bostoniak first made their attack. As the people ran and hid, our dogs tried to fight for us. They were too brave and too loyal to run. They had done no more than begin to sound the warning before their voices had been stilled forever. Their throats had been cut, their heads broken from the blows of clubs or tomahawks. That image came to my mind as I watched the geese. Their great V's became blurred by the moisture in my eyes.

The Worrier and I walked on. My hands were clasped together. My fingers kept tracing the surface of my ring. I could no longer feel the throb of pain from the wound in my shoulder. Perhaps the Worrier's medicine was doing its work or perhaps my body, too, was becoming as forgetful as my eyes and ears.

There were more voices around us. Those who had left town before the celebration were returning to see, with great shock, what had happened while they were gone. The fighting men of our village were coming back—those who had been searching for our enemies where Alsigontikuk runs into the great river that flows to the salt water. The Bostoniak had been too clever for them, and struck our village from behind. We had been outwitted by the White Devil.

The mouths of those fighting men of St. Francis were open as if they were shouting. I could barely hear their words. One of them grasped me by the shoulder, placed his face next to mine, and shook me. For a moment I felt again that pain in my shoulder, but the words he spoke made no sense to me. He let go of my arm and moved on.

I hardly noticed. I was looking now at the branch of a pine tree. Not just at the branch, but at its green needles. The pine is always green and does not lose its leaves like the maples or the birch trees. Its needles grow in bundles of five. When its cones fall upon the earth, small pines then grow beneath the sheltering branches of the big tree. There is a song that we sing about the little pines dancing. If you take one of those bundles of five needles and spread them apart, you can balance them on the head of a drum. When you tap that drum softly, the pine needles will dance.

As I looked at the pine needles, I thought about all the gifts the pine gives us. I thought of how you can make a tea from its needles that will drive away the winter cough. My mother had taught me that. Just this past winter she had made such a tea when both my sweet sisters were ill. Together we had nursed them back to health with the pine's gift. I thought of how the inner bark of the pine is good to eat. I thought of how we could use its wood for building our homes, squaring its trunk into beams; how it would keep us warm as we burned its dry limbs.

I saw fire in my mind then, and every painful thought I had tried to keep away from my heart came rushing back. My eyes closed. It seemed as if I fell forward a long, long way into darkness. But I did not fall far. When I opened my eyes again, I found myself on my knees. A torn-off branch of the pine was in my left hand and I was pounding the earth with my fist.

The Worrier stood there silently. When I was done, I looked up at him and he nodded at me.

"We will find them," I said to him.

11

COOKING FIRES

There was no longer any doubt about who our attackers had been. They were Rogers' Rangers. They had all worn the green caps of the Rangers and been dressed in buckskin. These were the same men who had been beaten so badly by our brave brother Sieur Langy Montegron and his party of Frenchmen and Indians. In that battle, fought a year and a half before on snowshoes near the great French stronghold at Fort Carillion, the Rangers had tried to ambush Langy. But he had turned the tables on them. For a time it had been thought that Rogers was among the many Bostoniak dead. But, to our sorrow, it was not so. Our great enemy had survived. Now he had struck at the very heart of our people.

A small group of women and children came running into the ruins of the village. The White Devil had set them free.

"I do not think he was being kind," one of the women said. It was Martha, the older sister of my friend Piel, whom, like Antoine, I had yet to see. I feared they were among the dead. There was such confusion that I wondered if we would ever know who had been taken captive and whose burned bodies were buried in the blackened ruins of our homes.

"He let us go," Martha said, "because so many of us had already escaped from him. He knew he would have to kill us to keep us from getting away."

"Some of those bad men would have been glad to kill us," said the little girl clutching Martha's hand. Her face was so blackened by soot that at first I did not recognize her as Alanis Nolette.

"The bad men were starving, so hungry that I thought they were going to eat us," Alanis said. "They went around pinching the arms of those of us who had been taken captive. They said they only wanted to take the fattest of us with them."

"It is so," said Esther, the mother of little Alanis. She placed one hand upon the shoulder of her daughter and the other on her own forehead—as if to reassure herself that they were both truly alive and free from those terrible men.

Esther had spent much time with Mrs. Johnson and could speak English well. When parties of our people went down to Fort Number Four to trade, Esther often accompanied them and did most of the talking. But she had not spoken any English to the Rangers. She had only listened. Now she described how strangely the Rangers had acted during their attack.

"I watched almost all of it from the place where my child and I were hidden beneath Ely's cabin. I saw the Stockbridge Indians come into town first, as if driven ahead of the Rangers. Maybe they hoped that their Indian scouts would draw the fire of anyone who was not surprised. Then the Rangers came in. While some were shooting, others were making fires and setting up pots for cooking! Whenever they broke down the door of a house, they would come running out with whatever food they had found and carry it to the cooking fires. Before the food was even half cooked, there would be a circle of men about it, grabbing at the food. They were like madmen, starving madmen. Or like dogs. They even dropped their spoons and ate with their hands. See."

She reached into her blouse and pulled something out. It was a pewter spoon. I realized now that I had seen several of those upon the ground as I walked about the village. I had also seen the remains of those cooking fires. Then Esther Nolette told us more of what she had seen and heard. In their hard march to our village, our enemies had foolishly lost their packs of food while crossing the river. They had been without any real food for days.

"Of all the men among our attackers," Esther continued, "the White Devil seemed to be the only one with real wisdom." Rogers had realized how few people were in a village that usually held twice as many. He knew that our French friends and our warriors would surely have heard the gunfire or seen the smoke from St. Francis. He had tried to find white people among the captives, people who could speak

English to him and give him information. He had given orders to his men to kill no women or children, though few listened to him when they were out of his sight. Still, the Bostoniak had kept some captives. Choosing people with blue or green eyes, they brought those who might be white to Rogers. Among them were Marie-Jeanne Gill, her two daughters, and her son, my friend Antoine.

As for Piel, no one knew for certain where he had gone after the Council Hall. Some thought they had last seen him in one of the houses that was burning. There had been such great confusion as Rogers and his men ransacked the town.

"The White Devil asked Marie-Jeanne where the warriors of our village were," Esther said. Then she smiled. "Marie-Jeanne looked straight into his eyes and spat in his face. Pah! 'They are behind you,' she said."

While his men tried to collect loot, Rogers strode among them, forcing them to drop what prizes they had taken, making them fill their empty packs with nothing but food. He and another of his officers checked their packs before they left, driving their captives ahead of them from the ruins of our village.

"Still," Esther said, "there were a few men who hung back, carrying heavier packs than the others. They were the ones who stole the silver from our church—the communion plate, the chalice, the candleholders. Even though their eyes were just as dark with hunger as the others', still their hunger for the bright metal overcame them."

I had waited as patiently as I could while Esther spoke.

Now I could wait no longer. "I cannot find my mother and sisters," I said. "Did you see them among those who were taken or . . ."—I took a breath as my words caught in my throat—"those who were released?"

Esther looked at me in confusion. It was as if she could not recognize me. Then I realized how I must look, with blood upon my clothes, and my face covered with soot. "It is me, Saxso. Did you see my mother or my sisters, Marie-Jeanne and Katrin?"

"Ah, Saxso," Esther said. Then she shook her head. "No, I did not see them. Were they not with you?"

12

PIECES COMING TOGETHER

Esther's words added to my weight of guilt. And as the Worrier and I continued to walk about the ruins of our village, a picture of what had happened to my family began to emerge. Each small part fit together like pieces of cloth that, when finally sewn, make a shirt. I tried to listen calmly. My parents had taught me to be calm and careful in times of great trouble. Becoming lost in guilt and grief is selfish and of no help to anyone.

Gabriel Annance told of how he went to his house to get his son and small daughter. They were alone there, for Gabriel's wife had died from a fever two winters before. He was upset with his son, who had not thought to load his gun. "You must always be ready in case enemies come," he scolded. Then Gabriel bade the children to run ahead of him, taking the path behind his house into the woods. But as his children set out along that path, Gabriel saw one of Rogers' green-bereted men moving through the brush. The Ranger was heading toward where the children would enter the forest.

"I dropped to one knee and shot at the man, and he disappeared," Gabriel said. "So my children got away."

Perhaps the man was wounded or just frightened by the shot and ran away, for no bodies of white men were found after the battle, only Samadagwis, who became Jean Baptiste.

Once Gabriel saw that his children were safely hidden, he had gone back into the center of town. He had been especially concerned about the safety of Marie-Appoline Gill. The sound of gunfire and the shouts of the battle were now loud. It was as confusing as being in the midst of a great storm. Perhaps it was one of those coincidences that sometimes happen in war. Or perhaps their spirits were so close that they drew them together, for almost immediately he found Marie-Appoline hiding near the trail.

"They have captured my family," she told him. That was all she said at first, as he took her to a safer hiding place. Gabriel paused then in his telling of the story to us.

"Saxso," he said, "she told me that she saw others besides her own relatives being taken. Among them were your mother and your two sisters."

Dauphine Sausiboite was among those who had been hiding in the ravine. "Your sister Marie-Jeanne," she said, "she kept asking what would happen to Antoine Gill back in the

Council Hall. Your mother kept saying that nothing could be done. So when your mother was turned away from her, Marie-Jeanne ran after you when you left with Great Simon. Then your mother told Katrin to wait for her and not move, and she ran after Marie-Jeanne. I held on to Katrin's arm to keep her from following. But you know that no one can ever tell anyone in your stubborn family what to do. As soon as your mother was gone, your little sister Katrin bit my hand and then twisted away from me to scramble up the bank and run after your mother."

Dauphine held up her hand to show me the marks of Katrin's strong teeth. "You see," she said, "she bites like a beaver, that sister of yours. I am sorry for the white men if they have taken *her* captive."

My heart sank. It was my fault that my family had been taken. Had I not deserted them in that ravine, I would have been there to stop them from leaving their place of safety. I closed my eyes, clenched my fists, and lowered my head in despair.

With my eyes closed, I heard new voices coming toward me. The voices were not speaking in Abenaki but in French, their accents not those of Indians. I lifted my head. Drawn from Yamaska by the sounds of battle and the columns of smoke that rose as high as the clouds from our burning town, the French soldiers had finally arrived.

A few were Marines. My uncle had taught me how to tell the difference between them and the Milice, the Colony Militia. "Look at their sleeves," Uncle Pierre had said. The turned-back gauntlet cuffs of the Marines' woolen waistcoats are blue. They wear long linen shirts and tricorne hats. Since the morning had been cold, some of them were wearing scarves under those caps. But the heat of their forced march had led many to use those scarves to wipe the sweat from their faces. Each man was equipped with a fine long-barreled fusil. Those French guns shoot a smaller, lighter ball than the English muskets. They are feared by the Bostoniak, who know the French are better shots than they.

The other Frenchmen were Milice. Militiamen are not professional soldiers from across the ocean but men of "New France," as they have renamed the part of our land where they have settled. So their appearance is quite different. Instead of the awkward tricornes, they wear woolen caps. Their coats have a single button at the top and are tied at the waist with a woolen sash. A few of the Militiamen had no coats at all and looked more Indian than French. Their leader was barechested. His face was painted like an Abenaki warrior. Blue streaks crossed his cheeks. His forehead was black and there were green circles around his eyes. Upon his bare chest hung the shiny brass gorget that marked him as the leader. It was none other than my father's old friend Langy.

There was a grim look upon the face of Sieur Langy Montegron. I imagined he was questioning his judgment in seeking the enemy elsewhere while the attack came on our defenseless village. He bent down by one of the fires that the Bostoniak had made to cook the food they stole from our homes. He picked something up and looked at it. It was a chewed musket ball. The English sometimes chew their musket balls before loading them into their guns. When a chewed ball strikes a person, it tumbles in the flesh and breaks into pieces when it hits bone, making a terrible wound. The French consider chewing musket balls a cowardly and dishonorable thing.

"Pigs," he said. "Dogs!" He threw the musket ball down and ground it into the earth with his foot.

As the Frenchmen followed the instructions of their leader, gathering information about what had happened, making ready for the pursuit of the enemy, the thirty or more Indian men with them paid those orders no attention. Their first concern was the safety of their families. They went about trying to learn who had been hurt or killed, who had survived, and who was missing.

My uncle Pierre Ktsi Awasos found me before I found him. He did not ask me what had happened; he only looked at me. My uncle is quick to understand any situation. My mother once said that I am more like her brother than anyone else. I consider this a great compliment. No one is stronger than Uncle Pierre, who is like the bear that gave our family its name. No one can run longer or follow a trail better. It is said that as an infant I went from crawling to running. Though I now had only fourteen winters, I was the biggest of the boys in St. Francis. But I had never used my size to bully those smaller than me. I had always hoped that I would grow to be like my uncle, known as a faithful hunter who hears the good spirit voice—a defender of our people. But I could not be that way now.

"My uncle," I said, holding my empty hands before me

like one who has dropped something precious and watched it shatter. "I have lost them. I have failed my mother and sisters."

Uncle Pierre held out his arms to me. Great warrior though he was, there were tears in his eyes. As I embraced him, we both wept.

13

THE SILVER VIRGIN

There is a confusion of voices and faces in my mind when I try to recall the rest of that awful day. It was like canoeing down a great river: calm one minute and awash with rapids the next. I would float along in moments of absolute clarity. Then everything around me would seem to spin and blur, as if I was caught in a whirlpool. Perhaps I was becoming feverish from my wound.

I remember walking with my uncle, talking with him about what had happened. I have no memory of the words I spoke, but I recall his calm, a calm like that of the sky just before it breaks into a powerful storm. As he listened to me, his eyes took in every detail of our destroyed village, burning it into his own mind so that it would never be forgotten.

There were three of us walking together as the sun rose higher above the horizon. Uncle Pierre was on my right.

Once he had been so tall that when he lifted me, it seemed as if I was going into the sky land. Now he was only a hand's width taller than me. On my left was the Worrier, small and round. Even when I was a child, I had not thought of him as a grown-up. Though he showed a serious face to the other adults, with the children he was like a child himself, always joining us in our games, making faces, and telling us funny stories. No laughter was in his face now. From time to time he looked up at me, appearing even more worried than usual. It almost made me want to laugh, though tears kept coming to my eyes.

I knelt to look at a piece of burned cloth that had once been part of a woman's dress. The pattern on that cloth was of blue and white flowers. I recognized it, and yet I could not recall who wore it. Half of the cloth was singed black from fire. I was confused. Everything that had been so familiar all of my life was now different. I pressed the burned piece of a dress to my face, wondering if I would smell my mother's perfume. I smelled only the scent of burned fabric. My uncle helped me to my feet, took the torn cloth from my hand, and placed it back upon the ground.

At some point, our priest returned. I do not recall coming to the remains of our church, but I must have done so. Father Roubaud stood there, his head down, his hands held out from his sides. It was much like the pose of our crucified Lord. He seemed to be waiting for the nails to be driven into his own palms.

"Gone," Father Roubaud said, speaking in French and using the same voice with which he preached. "Gone. The beautiful silver statue of the Blessed Virgin Mary that was sent fifty years ago by the Chartres fathers all the way from France. All of the ornaments of our little church."

Father Roubaud paused. Though he had not looked at us, I was sure that he knew we were listening. The silver virgin of St. Francis was regarded as a blessing upon our village. It had been visible proof of our ties to the French. It had been sent to us from far across the great water as evidence that we were the spiritual children of Mother France.

Father Roubaud took a deep breath. "Gone. All of the records of births and deaths, of marriages and confirmations. All stolen or burned by those godless English."

The Worrier leaned toward Father Roubaud.

"Blackrobe," he said in French, "more than paper and wood burned in that fire."

Father Roubaud took a step backward and shook his head. *"Ni-oloma-waldam-wo-ganak?"* he said haltingly, trying to put his words into Abenaki. "My faithful ones? Some of them were in the church?"

The Worrier held up three fingers in front of the Jesuit. He let his hand flutter toward the blackened earth like a maple leaf falling from a tree.

"Nhloak," the Worrier said. *"Tres."* Then he named them.

Father Roubaud flinched as each name was spoken. "I should have been with them," he said in French. His voice was very small now. "But the noise of celebration was so great last night that I could not sleep."

As we walked away from Father Roubaud, Uncle Pierre

shook his head. "He is not like our old priest, Father Aubery."

"He was my friend," the Worrier said. "I do not think he will stay here with us now."

"Not without his silver virgin," said my uncle.

"Awasos," the Worrier said, "my friend is only a French priest, but he was not just here for the silver." Then the Worrier looked upriver. "Some of the Bostoniak were. Instead of corn, they filled their packs with metal they cannot eat. That silver virgin, those plates and candlesticks. Hah! Their plunder will be heavy for them to carry. It will slow them down."

"We will catch them," my uncle declared. "They are on foot. We will go upriver by canoe."

"I will go with you," I said. Or at least that is what I tried to say. My words stuck in my throat before they reached my lips. The taste of blood and burning wood was in my mouth as I sank into a pool of darkness.

14

Two Days' Start

The taste on my lips was still warm and salty, but the smoke that filled my nose was healing smoke, not the scent of death. I opened my eyes. Bundles of medicine plants hung over my head. Shapes of birds and animals were incised into the bark roof. I was in the Worrier's lodge. He was lifting my head up with one hand.

"Where is my uncle?" I asked. My voice was so weak and cracked that I sounded like some small, featherless bird begging its mother for food. A wooden spoon filled with broth entered my mouth and I swallowed. I realized how hungry I was, hungrier than I should have been.

Finally, when the bowl was empty, the Worrier helped me raise myself up. He patted my shoulder where I had been wounded. I pressed my fingers against the already healing wound. There was barely any pain. I felt strong and rested.

"Sleep is one of the best medicines," he said.

"How long did I sleep?" I asked.

The Worrier looked at me as if trying to decide whether or not he should answer. I looked back.

He sighed. "I will tell you if you do not jump like a startled rabbit as soon as I have spoken."

"How long?" I insisted.

The Worrier held up his right hand in a fist. With his left hand, as if peeling the bark from a tree, he slowly uncurled first one finger and then another.

"Two days!" I shouted. I leaped up so quickly that I struck my head on the lodgepoles at the top of his small wigwam and immediately fell back down, grasping my forehead. I struggled to rise again. The Worrier's hands were on my shoulders, holding me down. His face was next to my ear.

"*Gigiktamo,*" he said. "Pay close attention." Then he called me by the name he had given me two winters ago: White Man Talker. "Awanocewodwa," he said, "sometimes you are too quick to act. Perhaps it is because you now have so many languages all talking to one another within your head. Perhaps those words of the Platzmoniak and Bostoniak sometimes make you think as they do, always restless and never listening. Now you *must* listen if you would do any good at all. Hear me. You want to save your family. You are not too late. Be patient, listen. I will help you."

I kept my mouth shut and did not try to rise. But I did hold up my hand and wiggle it back and forth. The Worrier snorted. "All right," he said. "One question. Only one."

"*Doni nizasiz?*" I said. "Where is my mother's brother?"

"Upriver," the Worrier said. "He has gone with Langy in pursuit of our enemies."

The Worrier closed his mouth like a turtle and stared at me. It was a test. If I said anything at all, I would fail. Words were fluttering about in my head like a flock of birds caught inside a wigwam. But I remained silent.

"*Wligen,*" the Worrier said. "Good. You will allow me to help you. Come now."

I followed the Worrier outside and looked up into the sky. From the position of the sun, I could tell it was midday. It was colder than it had been on the morning when the attack took place. Now there would be frost upon the ground each day. The small ponds would soon freeze.

The Worrier's wigwam was close to Alsigontikuk, and he took the narrow trail through the brush that led down to the water. There, just up from the river's edge, was a new birch bark canoe turned upside down. It was made in the way only our people can make a canoe. A single tree had furnished the double layer of bark that sheathed it. Spruce pitch had been melted and blackened with charcoal to cover the seams where smaller pieces of bark had been sewn together with spruce roots to form the front and back of the canoe. The rest—floor slats, thwarts, crosspieces, and braces—was made of carved and split cedar planks. This beautiful canoe was decorated with double curved designs all along its side. The shape of a leaping salmon was etched into the bark. I knew that sign. Uncle Pierre signed every canoe that he made. I had helped him make others like this one. But this was the finest I had ever seen.

The Worrier nodded. "Yes," he said. "Your uncle began work on this four moons ago. It was meant as a surprise. It is yours."

I knelt and ran my hands along its side. The canoe seemed to sing to me as I touched it. It was large enough to hold several people, but small enough for a single person to paddle upriver. With one hand, the Worrier turned the canoe right side up. Beneath it were not only the carved paddles, but also a pack and something else, partially wrapped in a deerskin. Exposed metal glinted in the sunlight.

The Worrier picked up the deerskin bundle, unwrapped it carefully, and handed to me what it held. It was a beautiful short-barreled French musket. Its brass was polished, every piece of it in order. The weight and balance felt perfect in my hands as I hefted it. It spoke of my uncle, who was careful and methodical in everything he did, especially when preparing to go hunting or to the field of battle. Those who were not ready were those who did not survive.

"Most battles are lost," Uncle Pierre had once said to me, as I watched him take his musket apart and put it back together again, "before the fighting ever begins."

I ran my hand over the smooth wood of the fusil's stock. Its trigger guard had been enlarged so that it could be fired in the winter without having to take off a mitten. It was a 1734 grenadier musket, a fine weapon. My eyes ran over every part of it, from the mainspring to the ramrod tip. I reached down and picked up the giberne, the shooting bag that held the rolled paper cartridges, the extra flints, the hammer stall, and vent picks. I slung it over my shoulder. The Worrier handed me the foumiment, the leather flask filled with powder. I hung it from my belt.

As I studied the musket, a single question came to my mind. Was I going to be allowed to pursue those who had kidnapped my family?

"My uncle . . ." I began to ask.

"He knows your stubbornness," the Worrier answered. "If he or I or anyone were to tell you not to follow this trail, it would only make you more determined to do so. So he decided, and I agreed, that the best thing to do would be to see that you were well-prepared. Much of what you will need is here. As for the rest . . ."

The Worrier stepped forward and placed his palm on my chest above my heart. He patted it four times and I nodded.

15

THE SHOULDER BONE TRAIL

Close to the river's edge a fire had been made in a circle of stones. The Worrier sat me down beside it.

"They have a start on you, but I will assist you. You will also help yourself, for you have only one purpose." He placed his hand upon his bare chest where the snake tattoo swam across. "I have spoken to my good spirit. That is what it tells me. If you go with one purpose, you will succeed."

The Worrier turned toward the sunset direction, the other side of the river where the woods were deeper. He whispered something under his breath too softly for me to hear. Then he nodded. "I have spoken to the Forest Dweller. He tried to warn us. Now he is filled with sorrow. He will leave this land. Our people will not see him again for many winters. But he, too, wishes to help you, Awanoce-wodwa. He says that the weapons you carry are not for killing human beings. You may hunt with them, your bow and arrows, your fine new gun. But you must not seek to kill other humans, even Bostoniak."

The Worrier squatted down by the fire. He began spreading out its coals—not with a stick, but with his bare hands. He brushed the red-hot embers with his palms as if smoothing out cool sand from the riverbank.

"The men of our village and our French brothers, their purpose is different. They seek to kill our enemies, to bring back their scalps. Perhaps that is not so true of your uncle, but the ones he travels with will sweep him along in that direction. You, however, will travel alone. Your purpose will be to rescue your family."

"I will remember," I said.

The Worrier unslung the bag hung over his shoulder, a bag not made of cloth, but woven in the old way from strips of soft basswood bark. He dumped its contents, half a dozen wide, flat bones, onto the sand. They were the dried shoulder bones of moose. Eager as I was to start on my journey, I leaned closer. I knew what he planned to do. Though I had heard of this, I had never seen it done before. He would show me the path I had to follow. He would read it in the cracks of the bones.

The most devout Catholics among our people frown upon this practice, just as they do not like to hear talk of good spirit helpers, the Forest Dweller, or the little people who live beneath the river. They say it is calling upon the devil. But they do not make fun of it. They do not try, like

Father Roubaud, to explain it away by saying that the Worrier chooses only the shoulder bones that already have cracks that fit the story he has decided to tell. Like my mother, I go faithfully to the church of the Jesuit fathers. I accept that Sazos Klist, Christian son of Ktsi Nwaskw, is good and great. But he was born far away and brought here by the French. Good and great things here in our old ways are also gifts of Ktsi Nwaskw, the Great Mystery. Sazos Klist surely knows this.

The Worrier looked carefully through his collection of shoulder bones, holding each one up in turn and running his fingers over its surface. If there were already cracks and lines in those bones, I could not see them. At last he chose one and placed it on the glowing coals. The hot, sharp smell of burning rose from the fire. The moose scapula made crackling sounds as it grew hotter. Finally, the Worrier plucked the bone out and dropped it between us. He rubbed a handful of sand across the surface, brushed it off, and studied the bone with great care.

"Ahhh," he said.

I waited.

"Kinawa," the Worrier said.

I looked. With one short finger, stubby as the toe of a bear, the Worrier traced a long line that led down the face of the shoulder bone.

"Our river," I said.

"Onh-honh," he answered. "You see clearly. That is the road you must travel." He pointed to the side of the crack.

"They are here, traveling by land. The Bostoniak now stumble through the swamps, growing ever more lost and ever more hungry."

I looked closer. I saw the fainter line that wound its way down the other side of our river, through the valley of Alsigontikuk.

"Here," the Worrier said, pointing to a wider crack in the shoulder bone, a crack that curved like a bow. "Memphremagog. Near the big swampy lake the white men will behave like foolish children. They will break up into smaller parties and try to find food. Here you will cross over. Beyond here you may find your family . . . if all goes well."

"I see it," I said. "But what is this?" I placed my finger on another long line farther to the south, a line like another river.

"Kwanitewk," the Worrier said. "The Long River." He looked at me and pursed his lips, as if about to say something. Then we both heard the distant sound of shouting coming from upstream by the ruins of St. Francis.

"The Mohawk Lover has finally come home from hunting," the Worrier said. "Let us go and see."

I began to pick up my things.

The Worrier shook his head. "Leave them here or you will find yourself traveling with him. Remember, your journey must be made alone, White Man Talker."

16

CHIEF GILL ARRIVES

When we reached the edge of the village, I saw a small cluster of men gathered together. In their center was Chief Joseph-Louis Gill. Before the raid, he had been one of the best-off men in our village. His house had been the finest. His wife, Marie-Jeanne, was the daughter of a beloved chief. She was one of the most admired of women. Their children had been well-behaved and respectful to elders. And now?

Now I saw before me a man whose sorrows were so heavy, they would have broken the back of a weaker person. His broad shoulders were hunched as if absorbing blows from a heavy club.

I looked around the remains of St. Francis. It was the

first time I had seen it in two days. The devastation was the same, but now I saw no more than a handful of people. I wondered where the other survivors had gone.

"Some of our people," the Worrier softly said to me, reading my mind as he so often did, "have gone to the other mission villages. One large party left yesterday afternoon for Akwesasne to live among the St. Regis Mission Mohawks. Others have gone early to their winter hunting grounds. They feel there is no safety here now."

"Your sister Marie-Appoline," Gabriel Annance was saying to Chief Gill, "she is safe. She is with my mother and sisters."

"What of my wife and my two sons?" Chief Gill said in a slow voice that seemed to caress their names. "Marie-Jeanne, Xavier, Antoine?"

No one answered him. His friends had already told him that his family was taken as captives, taken by the Rangers.

Chief Gill lowered his face into the cup of his hands and moaned. It was not a moan of despair. It was like the sound a bear makes before it charges, a low sound growing louder until it becomes a threatening growl. Everyone moved back half a pace. No one wished to be too close to Joseph-Louis Gill when he was truly enraged.

Many know the story about Chief Gill and his family—not only those of us in St. Francis, but throughout Canada. His name is legendary. His father, Samuel, and then his mother came among us as captives from different white settlements when they were children. When they were grown, they married. Their children, though white in skin, were deeply Indian at heart. Samuel had died only the previous year. He had lived to see his son become a war leader and respected *Sogmo,* one of the chiefs of the Abenaki.

Though born into our tribe, Joseph-Louis Gill's blonde hair and fair skin set him apart. Some had wondered openly if his heart could be truly Indian when his appearance was so clearly that of a white man. Nine years ago he had proven himself. He had volunteered to go on an expedition against the Miami, who threatened to wipe out our French brothers in their small outpost of Detroit near Mitsigami, the Great Lake. But according to my uncle, who was part of that company of French-Canadians and Abenakis led by Sieur de Beauharnais, Joseph-Louis Gill's bravery in battle was not the final proof.

"We were crossing a place where there were many flat stones," my uncle had told me. "Rattlesnakes were sunning themselves. Among them was a very large rattlesnake, its body as thick as a man's arm. Piel Sokoki began to tease Joseph-Louis. 'Mohawk Lover,' he asked, 'how are your teeth?' It was a way of saying to Joseph-Louis that he was not really Indian."

I understood. It is the old practice among our people, when our children have finally gotten their second set of teeth, to catch a green snake. The child must then bite along that snake's body all the way from the head to the tail. If a child does that properly, his teeth will always be strong, even in old age. That is why the teeth of Indians do not grow brown and weak and broken like those of white people. Because Joseph-Louis Gill's parents were both white captives, they had never caught a green snake for their children.

"Piel Sokoki took two forked sticks and pinned that big rattlesnake to the ground, its tail whirring angrily. 'Come on, Mohawk Lover,' he said to Joseph-Louis. 'Make your teeth strong.'"

My uncle had smiled at this. I smiled too. Knowing the stubborn courage of Chief Gill, I had already guessed what would happen next, though it was the first time I had heard the rattlesnake story.

"Joseph-Louis grabbed that big rattlesnake by the head and the tail, lifted it up, and crushed its spine with one bite. Then, as it writhed in his hands, he ripped open its body with his teeth, tore out its beating heart, and swallowed it."

Now Chief Gill raised his head, and there was a determination in his gaze that must have also been there the day he answered the challenge of the rattlesnake. He looked around our small circle, his eyes picking out several men who nodded back at him in turn. Before his eyes reached me, though, I looked down at the earth.

When I looked up again, Chief Gill and three others were already halfway to the river's edge. I watched as they slung their weapons and provisions into two canoes, shoved the prows into the river, and leaped in as lightly and swiftly as squirrels, two to a boat. Their paddles were in their hands and dipping into the water in less than a heartbeat, driving them swiftly upstream.

"I am sorry for the Bostoniak when he finds them," the Worrier said.

"I am not," I answered. "Let him eat their hearts."

17

SETTING OUT

Long ago, my mother told me, all rivers flowed in two directions. Along one bank the rivers flowed one way; along the other they flowed the opposite way. There was no upstream or downstream. It was as true for Alsigontikuk, our own river, as for all the others. One had only to paddle to one bank or the other to be carried by the current in the direction he desired. Rivers were made that way by Ktsi Nwaskw, the Great Mystery, to help the people.

All that Ktsi Nwaskw asked was that the people remember to be thankful. But people became too lazy. They took it for granted that it should be so easy to travel. They stopped being thankful. The Creator was not pleased. So things were changed. Now all the rivers flowed downstream. And rapids and waterfalls were placed to make things even more difficult.

When I heard that story as a small child, I felt resentful about those people who had forgotten to be thankful. My mother was standing behind me as I played in an eddy of the river. I had made a small canoe from a strip of birch bark and was watching it circle in the whirlpool created by the stones at the river's edge.

"How could they be so foolish?" I asked my mother, as I guided my canoe by gently pushing one side and then the other with a long twig. "It is the easiest thing in the world to just say thank you. How could anyone be so foolish as to forget that?"

My mother said nothing for a long time. Finally, I turned and looked up at her. She was smiling, but her face seemed sad. "Son," she said, "things sometimes happen to people as they grow older. I pray that it will always be easy for you to be thankful."

As I set out alone up the river, I tried to remember the words of thanks my uncle had taught me to speak when one departs on a journey. One must thank water and land— trails to be followed on *sibok,* the river, and *kik,* the earth. I tried to remember not only with my mouth but with my heart. It was not easy, but I tried hard.

I understood now what my mother meant that day when nothing in the world stood between me and thankfulness. I had experienced few things then that might make the eye of a person's heart grow clouded. Now, after a handful of winters, so many bad things had happened.

There had been the smallpox that swept like a dark wind

through our little town three years earlier. Many of our people had died. I had lost friends. There were boys and girls I had played with whose faces I would never see again in this lifetime. And when the brief time of peace ended and the wars began again, many men left our village to fight by the side of our French brothers. Many of them had never come back again. My own father had lost his life in that way. Now our village had been destroyed before my eyes, my closest friends lost or among the dead. My dear mother and my two sisters had been taken from me—and my own foolishness was at least in part to blame. Perhaps even now they, too, were among those whose feet walked the sky road.

Those things stood between me and thankfulness like a great chasm. It was not easy to make a bridge of words that might allow me to cross over to the other side. It was almost too much to bear, even if one believed what Father Roubaud had said to us after my father's death.

"*Bon Dieu* is testing your faith," he said. "Accept his wisdom and cast out sin from your hearts. Pray for forgiveness."

I shook my head. I could not think as Father Roubaud wished me to think. Nor could I fill my heart with bitter anger like Chief Gill. His face had been more like that of a wolf than a man when he left the village. It seemed he was more eager for revenge, for the blood of those Bostoniak Rangers, than to save his kidnapped wife and children. Now was not the time for me to kneel and pray . . . nor was it the time for me to allow wild anger to twist in my head. My uncle and the Worrier were right. I needed to concentrate only on rescuing those I loved. I had to point my eyes and my heart straight.

I rested my paddle in the bottom of the canoe and placed my hands on either side of the beautiful craft that my uncle had made for me. I felt the designs he had etched into the sides, the roughness of the birch bark, the places where the fall of branches had made shapes like those of birds with wide-spread wings. I breathed slowly, breathed with the bobbing of the canoe in the water, breathed with the water's flow.

"Help me," I whispered.

Then I dug my paddle into the water. As I did so, I began to sing very softly. It was an old song taught to me by my father, one he said our river loved to hear.

> *Kwey–hey, kweh yoh hey hey*
> *Kwey–hey, kweh yo ney*
> *Kwey–hey, kweh yoh hey hey*
> *Kwey hey yo ney*

As I sang, I felt the river listening to me. I began to move more swiftly. I avoided the rocks and chutes of swift water. I kept my canoe close to the shore, finding the places where the current remembered the old days when it flowed in both directions. In those places the water was as calm as the surface of a pond. At times it even pushed me upstream. Or was it the small hands of the little underwater people speeding me along, recognizing not only my song but the designs on my canoe that marked me as a friend? I did not look down into the water to see if they were there. That would have been impolite. But I put them into my thoughts also as I continued to paddle. Despite the wound in my shoulder, I did not feel weak. Instead, I felt a strength I had never felt before.

I knew that I would be tired. I hoped that I would sleep deeply that night. I would continue paddling in this way without stopping for as long as the sun still shone down to touch the water of our river. The warmth of the sun was on my shoulders. Its bright light shaped a trail ahead of me, shimmering upstream like a wide band of silver. I felt grateful for the strength I had been given. I would rescue my family. I would not fail.

I rounded the bend above our village, the place where St. Francis can no longer be seen. Before, whenever I traveled this way, I had always looked back. I did not do so today. I kept my eyes forward.

A swallow dove down out of the sky and began to fly just ahead of me, its wingbeats matching the rhythm of the quick, even strokes of my paddle.

"My mother," I whispered. "My sisters. I am coming."

18

EMPTY SHORES

My uncle once told me that there is a sort of energy given to you when you go into battle—a strength that comes from such powerful emotions as fear and anger. It fills your body with warmth and certainty. You feel as if no enemy can touch you. No weapon can pierce your skin. Even when wounded, you feel no pain, but fight on forcefully until the battle is over. However, when the excitement of the fighting is done, that energy leaves you. You become weak and sick.

"Be careful of that reckless strength," my uncle told me. "It will not last. It may take more from you than it gives."

As the sun went down, I thought of those wise words of my uncle's. I had, indeed, felt such an energy as I set out upon the river. I was angry with the Bostoniak Rangers. I was fearful for the safety of my family. I felt as people do when they drink the bitter medicine water of rum.

All through that morning, I had no doubt about my success. I was as tireless as the swallow that flew ahead of my canoe. I did not pause to eat or even drink until the sun was in the middle of the sky. Then I took only a small handful of corn and a palmful of water from the river. That powerful energy stayed with me through the day.

When the shadows began to lengthen, things changed. The first doubts crept into my mind like the darkness that was deepening among the hemlocks and spruces near the river. Would I be able to find the trail of the Bostoniak who had stolen my family? Would they do harm to my mother and my sisters before I could find them? Would I be able to rescue them when I did find them?

Each of those thoughts was like a small drop of water escaping through a crack in the wall of a pot. Although the drops were small, they were many and did not cease. By the time the sun vanished below the trees and darkness spread its wide wings over the river, my pot of hope and certainty was nearly empty.

I pulled in where a sandbank at the base of a small rise showed me there had once been a village. That village had vanished from the riverside before I was born. Its bark houses had gone back into the earth. The drying racks where fish had been hung up to smoke and preserve had long ago been knocked down by the rising ice of winter, washed away by the floods of spring. Yet I could tell what a fine place this had once been for a village.

My arms and my back ached as I pulled my canoe out of the river. I was weary to the bone, but I had more to do. Instead of simply overturning my canoe near the water, I carried it on my shoulders farther up from the river and placed it upside down behind a small hump of land where there was a stand of hemlocks. I cut more hemlock branches to cover it. I took another branch and used it to brush away my tracks in the sand. As I did so, I tossed sticks and leaves and pebbles behind me so that I would not leave a smooth trail. "A wise person covers his tracks," the Worrier once said to me, "a foolish one simply wipes them away, making a smooth area more visible than the tracks he erased."

When I stood back a few feet and looked, there was no sign of my canoe and no trace of my passage up from the river. I had walked farther inland, beyond the village site, to cut the hemlock boughs that covered my canoe. Seeing branches cut from the trees by the river would be another giveaway to the eyes of a clever enemy.

I had already placed my pack and my few supplies under the canoe. All that I had carried with me as I made my shelter were my trade hatchet and my gun. I got down on my knees and crawled between the spruce boughs, under my canoe where other boughs that were spread on the ground would serve as a bed. I would make no fire. Its smoke would be visible for a great distance here along the river. Though it was growing colder with the darkness, I would not freeze. I would sleep wrapped in the wool blanket I had brought with me.

I was so tired. I thought that sleep would come to me in a heartbeat. But it did not. Instead, so many thoughts fluttered through my mind that I felt as if I was in the midst of one of those great flocks of pigeons that darken the sky when they travel past St. Francis every spring and fall. When those pigeons land in the trees nearby, there are so many that you can hear the sound of branches cracking under their weight. Those small, fat birds are very good to eat, and we always go out to hunt them with long poles, knocking them from the branches as they roost.

But I could not eat the thoughts that weighed me down that first night. Not only did I think of my family but also of the empty banks of this river. Once, a generation before, there had been many villages along the river. Now from St. Francis far upstream to Lake Memphremagog, only our village remained. The people had fled north to save themselves from the anger of the Bostoniaks.

As those thoughts came to me, it seemed for a moment as if I could hear the voices of the people who had once lived near this place where I sheltered beneath my birch bark canoe. Their voices were sad as they left their homes for the last time. They left behind not only their homes, the familiar land, the trees, and flowing streams. They also left their ancestors, buried in this earth. A great sorrow came over me at the thought of those old ones now forgotten. How empty this land is without our people here to give thanks, to welcome each new season.

I wondered once again why the hearts of the Bostoniak were so cold. Why did they want everything for themselves? Why were they unable to share this land with us, this land that held the bones of our people, this land that gave us our lives for generation after generation? Would St. Francis now be the same, a place of sumac trees where once there were the cabins of our people? Perhaps St. Francis, too, would be nothing more than an empty place beside the river where children no longer laughed and families no longer gathered to share food and give thanks.

Those were the thoughts—the questions for which there were no answers—that filled my head and kept me from sleep. The ache in my shoulder returned, and throbbed like a second heart. Every part of my body, even the hair on my head, hurt. How had I ever been foolish enough to think I could save my family? I was too small, too weak. My fingers, which had been grasping the canoe paddle all day, felt as numb and stiff as sticks of wood. Sticks.

I was feeling sorry for myself. I had not felt so sorry for myself since the day when I was a very small child playing by the river and I stepped on a sharp stick. It cut deeply into my foot and I ran to my mother, crying and leaving bloody footprints behind me. She had cleaned the wound and stopped the bleeding.

"You will be fine now," she had said to me.

But that did not satisfy me. I was feeling angry and betrayed by the fact that I had been hurt. I had done nothing wrong. I did not deserve to be hurt.

"No," I said, "I will not be fine. This is the worst thing that has ever happened to me."

I remember how my mother smiled then. *"Wli,"* she said. "That is very good. I hope that is so."

This made me more angry. "What do you mean?" I demanded.

"My son," she said, "if cutting your foot on a stick is the worst thing that will ever happen to you, then you will have a very happy life, indeed."

I was so stubborn that I did not even try to understand her words. "What could be worse than this?" I cried.

"Well," my mother said, "you could have stepped on two sticks."

Two Sticks. That, in fact, had become my nickname. I am not sure who overheard that conversation between my mother and myself. Perhaps it was one of my older cousins. By the end of that day, everyone knew the story, and my new name had been well-established. For the next four winters, until Mrs. Johnson came among us, Two Sticks was what everyone called me. It was only then that my nickname was replaced by Awanocewodwa, White Man Talker.

Remembering that story, seeing again the smile that was on my mother's face as she tried to teach a stubborn son, made me want to laugh and cry at the same time. All the feelings of self-pity left me. There, on that empty shore, I felt strength come back into my body and my heart. It was not the reckless strength that deserts you just as quickly as it arrives. It was a strength as quiet and as faithful as the firm guidance my mother always gave me. It did not come from anger or fear. It came from love.

19

HIDDEN CANOES

As I continued up the St. Francis, one sunset blurred into another. I ate sparingly from the food I had brought with me. The years of training from my uncle and other older men had taught me that it is not wise to fill your belly when you are on a long trail. Food was also constantly being given to me. The river was filled with fish. I had only to drop in a hook and line to bring out a fat bass or trout, meat I could eat without cooking.

Our northern land may seem barren to those whose eyes are only used to the sight of villages, but there is food to be found everywhere. The inner bark of the pine trees is good to eat and may be ground into a powder. It was past the season when blackberries and blueberries could be found, but there were many kinds of roots that could be dug from the earth or pulled from the base of such plants as the arrowroot that grows in the rivers and ponds.

On the fourth day of my journey, I rounded a bend in the river and found myself in the midst of a small flock of geese. It would have taken only one blow from my canoe paddle to kill one particularly fat and foolish male goose. As he ran on top of the water to escape, he was so close that I had to lean my head to the side to keep from being hit in the face by one of his wildly flapping wings. But I did not kill him. I still was avoiding the making of a fire, and I am not partial to the taste of raw goose. I did not need to take his life to sustain my own. Though it is not a Catholic tenet, I had been taught from childhood the ancient belief that it is a sort of sin to kill any game animal or bird that you do not intend to use fully.

Deer often came down to the water to drink when it was late in the day. I could have brought down a buck or doe with one shot from my rifle. But the sound of a gun, even more than the smoke of a fire, would have been like a signal to an enemy. "Here I am, I am foolish. Come and get me." Just before sunset, on the fifth day of my paddling, a fat doe who had no fawn by her side came so near, I could have struck her with a stick. She stood, her head raised, as I paddled by. When I looked back, she was still there, watching my progress.

As I traveled up the river, I saw the signs of others who had gone ahead of me. Perhaps it was my uncle and the French, led by Langy. Or perhaps it was the canoes of Chief Gill's party. Whoever it was, they had not shown the same caution as I had. I saw the remains of fires, the places by the river where branches had been cut, tracks that had not been covered. The moccasin tracks, by their shape, were made by our people. Every type of moccasin leaves a different shape, especially in the sand of a riverside. I understood why those ahead of me had not taken any care to conceal themselves. They were looking for a fight, inviting the enemy to come to them.

I carried my canoe over the portage and entered Lake Memphremagog. I had yet to see another human being, but I continued to eat lightly, to make no fires, to travel as swiftly as I could. I was growing more and more worried.

Late in the afternoon of my eighth day of travel, ten days after St. Francis was burned and my family captured, I found the canoes. I carried in my memory the map that the Worrier had shown me on the shoulder bone. The trail he had pointed out to me on the fire-blackened surface of the bone was the farthest to the west. So it was that I had chosen this route.

I pulled my own canoe up onto shore, where I saw the partially concealed drag marks of two canoes. I knew that the marks had been made at least two days earlier from the pine needles that had fallen into the tracks and the footprints of raccoons that crossed and recrossed them. It took only a few steps to locate the canoes that had been quickly hidden a little ways up the bank. I recognized the markings on the larger one. It was the canoe of Chief Gill.

A tamarack tree grew from the small knoll just above the boat. Unlike its relative the pine, the tamarack loses all of its needles in the fall. My mother once told me that the tamarack, pine, cedar, and spruce were given the word, soon after their creation, that they must stay awake for many nights. If they did so, they would be given a special power. On the last night of their test, only the tamarack fell asleep. The other trees were given the power to stay green all through the year, but the sleepy tamarack now must always give up its needles and stand bare through the whole winter. So many of those golden needles had fallen on Chief Gill's canoe that it almost seemed like a part of the little hill.

For some reason, the sight of that canoe covered with needles brought back to me again the feeling of great sadness that had weighed my heart at the start of my journey and touched me from time to time as I saw our old village sites along the river. The work of traveling up the St. Francis had taken that weight of sorrow away from me for a time. But now it was back.

Our people have lost so much, I thought. *We are as bare as the tamarack.*

Despite the heaviness of my heart, my ears were still alert. I heard the sound of feet approaching. They were moving downhill toward the canoes and the river. I ran swiftly back through the brush and concealed myself. Soon I saw them. Four men were coming down the hill. Their faces were painted red, an ancient sign among our people that a man is going into battle. But their shoulders seemed bowed and they dragged their feet; there was no victory in their steps. Each man carried more than one gun, and two of them were heavily laden with unfamiliar-looking packs.

"Nidobak," I called out to them in Abenaki, without showing myself. "My friends. It is me, Saxso from St. Francis. The one who was called Two Sticks."

So I spoke to make certain they would know exactly who I was and not think me an enemy pretending to be a friend by speaking our language. Even so, despite the weariness they had shown, all four men were either on their bellies or behind a tree with their weapons aimed in my direction before I had finished my words. They were old warriors. One did not live to be an old warrior without showing care.

"Awani wiji?" Chief Gill called. "Who is with you?"

"I am alone," I said. Then I stood up.

One by one Chief Gill and the others also stood and came over to me.

The fact that I am so well-known for my stubbornness may explain why they did not ask any further questions of me. That I would follow them all alone, even after being wounded in my shoulder, was no surprise to any of the men. But if they had no questions for me, I had some for them.

"You found the Bostoniak," I said, though it was not truly a question. The evidence was there in the extra guns they carried and the packs that had once belonged to Rangers. The dark stains on those packs had to be blood. They had been taken in battle.

The four men looked at me. They said nothing with their mouths, but the grim look in their eyes spoke more than words. The Worrier had been right to say that he pitied any Bostoniak Rangers caught by Chief Gill and his men.

I hesitated, knowing the question I wanted to ask and dreading the reply. Chief Gill's eyes were on me now. I took a deep breath.

"What of the captives?" I said.

"Dead," Chief Gill said, dropping his eyes to the ground as he spoke. His voice was slow and lifeless. "All of them. My wife and my two sons. Marie-Jeanne, Xavier, Antoine. They were killed and eaten by the Stockbridges and the Rangers."

20

STORIES OF BATTLE

I sat alone by the lake shore. With a willow stick held in my left hand I moved small stones and sand about. I made long lines in the shore that led to the water, patterns like the shapes of rivers and streams. After tracing each channel I would finally break the small gravel dam at its convergence with the river. Then I would watch the water flow into it the way a dry riverbed fills again when a beaver dam is broken. It was a game I could play all day in those years when I was small and there was no war. I would go to my special place above the rapids with a stick just like this one. I would imagine myself to be a giant looking down on the land from high above. Sometimes, during the long days of summer, I would remain even after the sun had begun to set. My mother or my father would have to come and tell me that they had saved food for me from the evening meal.

The sun was now only a hand's width from setting. It had moved the width of two hands across the sky since Chief Gill and his three companions had pushed off from this same shore and gone back toward the north, back toward the ruins of St. Francis. I had waded into the water and smoothed away the marks made by their canoes, even though there was no good reason for me to do so. Then I had sat down with my stick. I could think of nothing else to do. It seemed as if I would never again think of anything else to do. I had failed my family.

The stories that Chief Gill and his companions had told kept echoing in my mind. Three days before, Chief Gill and his party had met one small group of Rangers, three men lost from their main party. The fight with them had been short and fierce. None of the three Bostoniak Rangers survived or even lived long enough to answer any questions Chief Gill might have asked. But the look of those white men—gaunt faces, torn clothing, packs empty of food—had told a story of hunger and hopelessness. The Bostoniak were running from us and our French brothers like rabbits from wolves. In foolish desperation, they had separated into several parties in the rough lands west of Lake Memphremagog.

Chief Gill and his men had met other parties of our people. Each had their own tales to relate. One told of a battle in which two Bostoniak officers and more than a dozen other white men were wiped out without a single casualty on our side. Others spoke about capturing starving Bostoniak Rangers. All but one of those captive white men had

.been sent back under guard with the French. The awful story of that one white man made me shiver.

Our people had searched the man's heavy pack after taking him captive. They had seen the man trying to hide it from them. They hoped it held our church's silver statue of the Virgin Mary. Instead, they found the head and arm of a human being. Like one of the winter people from our old stories, that white man had butchered one of our people for food. When they turned their shocked eyes to look at the white man who owned that pack, he grinned at them and nodded his head in a crazy way. In horror and disgust, they killed him.

Another party of our people had gone to the Nulhegan River following the trail of the Bostoniak. That party told Chief Gill about his family. "We are sorry," they said. "Your wife, Marie-Jeanne, the beautiful one, is dead. Your two children, they are dead. They were killed like a doe and her fawns, and then eaten."

The main party of Rangers had not yet been caught. Rogers, the White Devil himself, was among those men. Under his leadership they were less foolish and harder to catch. It seemed they were still heading south, going down the Long River. Perhaps they hoped to meet reinforcements or make it all of the way to Fort Number Four. But there were no women among them, Chief Gill was informed.

He could bear it no longer. He had turned his face away. He could not help his lost loved ones. As a chief, he told me, he now had to think of those who had survived. He had to go back to St. Francis. He had been on that going-back trail when we met, returning to a home that would never again be the same for him. Nor would it be for me. I had lost everything in the world that mattered to me.

Yet as I sat there, making patterns with my stick, a small thought crept into my mind. Its track was as faint as that of a little bird hopping on the sand, but it became clearer as I studied it. I did *not* know for certain what had happened to my own family. I only knew what had been reported about Chief Gill's wife and his children. Were even those reports to be believed?

Deep in my mind I began to hear my uncle's calm voice. "Never base your actions on the first reports from any battle. There is always great confusion in war. The early stories brought back from any fighting are often wrong."

I looked at the lines of rivers and streams I had shaped with my stick. Without thinking, I had duplicated those patterns the Worrier had shown me on the moose shoulder bone. The place where my stick touched was the shore I had reached. I realized, as I looked at the pattern I had traced, that I had almost made a mistake. The trail the Worrier had shown me did not go to the southeast below Lake Memphremagog. It turned off toward the west, passing below the lake. Perhaps, when the Bostoniak Rangers broke up into smaller parties, one group, with captives among them, went to the west, toward the British stone fort at Crown Point.

I would not turn around in despair as Chief Gill had done. I had not yet reached the end of my trail. I would continue to seek my family. But I would not go in the direction taken by the White Devil.

21

THE KNOTTED BRANCH

To those who do not know the mountains and forests of our land, travel through them can be both frightening and confusing. Hills rise and fall, and thickets of intertwined tree limbs and sharp-thorned blackberry bushes are like walls to stop the progress of a traveler or turn one about in circles. So it seemed to have been for many of the Bostoniak in their flight from St. Francis. But it was not so for those of us who followed them. These were our old hunting grounds. Our villages had been here before a century of wars made the land no longer safe for our children and our elders. Where the Bostoniak blundered into swamps, we knew the firm ground to follow. Where they struggled to cross ridges and mountains, we took the passes between the high places and climbed to lookout spots that gave us a wide view of landmarks as familiar to us as signposts are to the white people.

It was on such a high spot of ground that I now stood. I had traveled all through the night down and across the lake. On the western side of the south bay I found the outlet to the Black River and went down it. At a certain place I hid my canoe and slept briefly before continuing on my way. There is a trail that leads toward Lake Champlain that is well-known to us. It was much traveled in the years before this last war began. We often followed that trail to trade with the English. If Stockbridge Indians were guiding the Bostoniak Rangers, they would follow this trail there in the notch below me.

I made my way down the slope, zigzagging back and forth to stay concealed as much as possible by the trees. Only a foolish person comes straight down a slope when there might be enemies about. The trail, like most of the ancient paths, was well-worn—not only by the feet of people but also by moose and deer and other animals that are as eager as humans to take an easier way. The first human prints I found were a day old. They had been crossed by the feet of a wolf that followed the trail a short ways before turning off into the brush. I took the wolf's tracks as a sign. Among our people a man who is a good hunter or a fine scout is brother to the wolf. My brother was showing me that this was the right path.

As I moved swiftly down that trail, I found other signs. More than one person had passed here. Bostoniak Rangers were among them. Where the earth was soft I saw the unmistakable tracks made by the boots of white men. The scuffing and dragging of feet that showed itself in some tracks, the broken twigs along the way, the place where someone had clearly fallen on top of a blueberry bush, crushing its branches, proved that some among them were careless or deeply weary. The poorly-covered remains of a fire was another sign of carelessness. I thrust my hands into the blackened remains of that campfire and felt no heat. This fire had not been made the night before.

I continued to follow the trail, looking for other signs. I recognized the shapes of Stockbridge moccasin tracks, but there were others. Some of the footprints were small and looked to have been made by a familiar set of moccasins, but I was not certain. Late on that day, I came upon a stream of clear water that flowed close to the trail and made a little pool. Those I was following had stopped there to drink. The water was so inviting that I stopped and drank from it myself and washed my sweaty face. As I lifted my head to look back up at the trail, I saw something in a low hemlock branch to one side. I quickly climbed up the slope from the pool to look closer and be certain my eyes had not deceived me. My heart leaped. Someone had quickly twisted the end of that branch, making a knot in it.

My fingers trembled as I touched the knotted branch. I knew who had left this sign for any rescuer who might follow. Though my father and uncle had taught me the most about the forest and its ways, someone else had first shown me how to leave this sort of trail marker.

I had been only five winters old on that warm summer

day in the forest. I had asked my mother how one kept from getting lost.

"There are many trails," I said to her. "What if I become separated from you while we are out berry picking? How will I know which trail to follow to find you?"

With a motion so quick that you could barely see it, hardly pausing as we walked along, she had reached out, pulled a slender branch toward her, and then released it. "Look back," she said.

I did so and saw that she had knotted the tip of the branch into a perfect circle. It was a circle as neatly made as the one I now traced with my fingers nine years later.

"Mother," I whispered, "I will find you."

22

THE SMELL OF MEAT

I smelled them before I saw them. I was moving slowly as I followed the trail. There was always the chance they would have a man hanging back, watching for pursuers. I remembered my uncle's story of the ambush set by the Rangers at Trout Brook near Fort Carillion. My father and my uncle Ktsi Awasos had been among the men at that battle. My father had been around the other side of the big hill with his friend Langy while my uncle was walking the ice trail upon the frozen surface of Namagokzibos, Trout Brook, scouting ahead of a line of 100 men under the command of Sieur de la Durantaye. He had found the tracks of enemy snowshoes and so was watchful. Still, he would not have survived that day had it not been for his spirit helper.

As he shuffled slowly along, that ancient sound of *ni-waskolalomo,* the good spirit voice, spoke to him in his head.

"Something is wrong. Stop and pretend to retie your snow-shoes." As soon as he did so, a musket shot was fired and the ball went over his head. My uncle and his men scrambled for shelter, but many fell as forty Brown Bess muskets let go. The snow was reddened by French and Indian blood. Then the screaming green-jacketed Rangers were upon them, wielding tomahawks and knives. Those of our people who could run took to their heels.

But the Rangers made a mistake. They stopped to take scalps, not noticing that our people had only run far enough to re-form and point their own weapons at the Rangers. Bostoniak fell as our warriors fired. Then Langy and his men, having heard the battle, attacked the Rangers from the other direction.

In the fight that followed, the Rangers were almost completely wiped out. "Our anger at the way they had taken the scalps of our fallen men drove all thoughts of mercy from our hearts," my uncle had told me. "So we took their scalps, more than one hundred forty of them. When darkness came, we allowed those few who had gone into the forest to escape. The White Devil was among them. There was a full moon and we could see their tracks. But to follow an armed man through thick brush at night would have been the act of fools."

Knowing my uncle's story, I stayed low as I followed and hoped that my father's spirit helper was with me. I also carefully watched for those places where men might lie concealed in wait. A full day had passed since I first saw the circled branch. I had found other of my mother's signs since then.

The trail was fresher now and the tracks told me many things. It was not a large party, no more than fifteen people. The shapes and sizes of their moccasins, the length and pattern of their gaits, had spoken. I recognized the moccasin prints of my mother and my two sisters. Similar sets of prints belonged to other women from St. Francis. From the depth of my mother's tracks, she was carrying a heavy load.

Darkness was closing over the trail. I would soon have to pause in my pursuit. The sky was clouded; the moon would be gone this night. A light evening wind was in my face. Oak and beech trees near the trail edge rattled their leaves in the breeze. Then I smelled it. Meat cooking.

A stand of hemlocks was ahead of me on one side of the curving trail. I crawled on my stomach through the hemlocks, whose branches were as low and wide as the skirts of a French woman. I made little noise over the cushion of needles, and the rattling of the dry leaves along the trail covered whatever sound I did make. Slowly as a mountain lion stalking an unwary deer, I crept closer and closer until I reached the ridge top.

It was good that I took such care. The trail was no more than a stone's throw below. Peering down through the screening branches of a hemlock, I saw a circle of people gathered around a fire made in a sheltered place along the trail. Blackened stones showed that other fires had been made there before. Five in that circle were white men. Their beards, green berets, and ragged clothing marked them as Rangers. They did not look gaunt and hungry; these men had been eating. Seeing the others in the circle around the fire, I knew why. The four other men were Stockbridge Indians, seasoned warriors who would not panic in deep forest, experienced hunters who would remember how to find food. Unlike the Rangers, the four Indians sat facing away from the fire, each looking in a different direction. It was a wise thing to do when enemies might be about. When you face the fire, its light makes you blind to anyone who might be approaching from the dark.

Six women and two children sat close to the fire. The two children were my sisters. Although their faces were dirty and their hair was tangled, they were alive. But not happy. I saw a wound on the side of my sister Marie-Jeanne's sullen face where someone or something had struck her. My mother was cooking as Katrin helped.

From the look and smell of the roast, dripping fat onto the coals from a spit, I could tell it was venison. My breath was slower and calmer than it had been when that first scent of meat drifted to me on the wind. Silly though my fears may have been, Chief Gill's words about his wife and children being eaten were still with me. I had dreaded what I might see. Perhaps I should have remembered that our enemies sometimes said that we Abenakis were cannibals. It is easy to imagine that those who go to war against you are the worst sort of monsters.

As I watched, I saw that my mother had kept her spirit. My sisters were close to her. As she did the cooking, she would turn first to one and then to the other of them. Her fingers untangled their hair, her hand gently wiped the dirt from their faces. None of them smiled, but I knew that my mother's strength kept sunshine in their hearts. She would never give in to despair. *Perhaps,* I thought, *one day I will have as much courage as you, my mother.*

I recognized the other five women there by the fire. All had come to us recently as captives. Three were liked in our community. The other two were different. The younger had blonde hair. The older woman's hair was the color of autumn oak leaves. Though many other captives learned to fit in, neither of those two was ever content among us. They resisted learning our language. No one was unkind to them, but no one became their friend. So they worked as servants in our village. They were fed well and clothed and given places to live. When they worked, they were paid for their efforts. But their hearts never opened.

They would have been traded back to the Bostoniak or sold to the French, who might have convinced them to join the true faith and enter a convent. Now the two women were on their way back to their own people. But they looked no happier. Were they having second thoughts about returning? Our friend Mrs. Johnson had worried about being fully accepted when she was redeemed to her people.

"Why is this so?" I had asked.

"The Bostoniak," my mother replied, "think that when a woman of their people has lived among us, it has made her unclean."

I wondered what I should do next. Not only did I have to worry about the Rangers and the Stockbridge Indians, but those two Bostoniak women would surely sound the alarm if they saw me.

What would my uncle have said? Wait. Do nothing quickly. So I kept watching, making no motion at all, breathing softly and slowly as the evening turned into night. I had already blackened my face with charcoal from the first cooking fire I found along the trail. I squinted my eyes as I watched so that no light would reflect from them. Still, careful as I was, it was almost not enough. Though I did not realize it at first, had I moved even one hand at the wrong time, it would have meant the end of my life.

23

THE STALKER

Although I am large, not only for my age, but even among the grown men of our people, I have always been able to move quietly in the forest. You may ask why this is so, but it should be no surprise. After all, those who make the most noise in the woods—aside from white people—are the small ones, the squirrels and chipmunks. You seldom hear a bear moving through the forest.

Our family has a special relationship with the bears. Long ago, one of my ancestors was stolen by the bears when he became separated from his mother while picking berries. The mother bear's cubs had been killed by an unwise hunter. So she stole that boy to take their place. She cared for him just as if he was a bear cub. He lived with the bears in their cave for some time before he was finally rescued by a hunter more clever than the others. Even after he was returned to his human family, my ancestor still thought he was a bear. It was several seasons before he again talked and acted like a person. Every generation of my family since then has always been close to the bears.

Quiet as I had been, someone in that party of Rangers and Indians must have heard a stray sound as I approached. Perhaps it was not even a noise that I had made. I had just been unlucky enough to come upon them at that moment. The watchful pose of those four Indians around the fire told me so. As did another sense besides sight or smell or hearing, a sense that made the hairs stand up on the back of my neck. That sense told me that another member of the war party was somewhere out away from the fire. Someone was hunting for whatever had made that stray sound. Hunting for me.

I lay motionless for a long time. The sky began to clear. For the first time since darkness had fallen, stars could be seen through the gaps in the trees. I did not look up at the stars to greet the little far-above ones, as I would have on any other night when I first saw them appear. I kept my eyes focused ahead of me and, though I did not move my head, to both sides. My gun was by my elbow, but it would do no good if an enemy found me here. My metal tomahawk rested lightly against my left side. Its blade, folded around a maple handle, was strong iron with an edge of tempered steel. I could whip my hand back and reach it in one motion almost as swift as a rattlesnake's strike. I could throw it with my left hand with such accuracy that I could strike the center of a small target at twenty paces. My favorite knife hung from its rawhide cord around my neck. A longer-bladed French knife was fastened to my calf. Neither of those were for throwing, but for fighting with an enemy who has closed in. I hoped that it would not come to tomahawk and knives. But I was ready.

As I listened, I began to hear a sound. It was a soft shuffling to my left, and it was coming toward me. *Oh, no,* I thought. I knew what that sound was. It did not represent a danger in itself. But the one making that sound might draw danger toward me.

Shuffle, shuffle, up the hill toward me. *Shuffle, shuffle,* heading right for my hiding place. Then I heard a softer noise, a moccasined foot being pressed down slowly as the man wearing that moccasin stalked in from the other direction, moving to intercept that shuffling sound. Another cautious footstep. The stalker was no farther than an arm's length away from me. I could hear his slow breathing.

I tensed my left arm, ready to reach back for my weapon.

"Unnnghhhhh?"

The moaning voice of the shuffling porcupine broke the silence. It was so loud, so ridiculous, that it almost made me laugh, despite the danger I was in.

"Unnnghhhhh?" the porcupine moaned a second time, shaking a small sapling with its front paws. This time its call *was* answered by laughter, not from me but from one of the three Stockbridge Indian watchers by the fire.

"Cheeksaunkun," a man by the fire called out, "come back now. You have saved us from attack by that porcupine."

My view of the stars was suddenly blotted out as the man

who had been stalking toward me stood and turned to face down the hill.

"My brother Jacob," Cheeksaunkun replied, his voice also choked with laughter, "you do not understand. It is a *big* porcupine."

He went back down the hill to the fire and I began to breathe again.

The five Bostoniak Rangers seemed uninterested in what had just gone on. Cheeksaunkun and Jacob had carried on their conversation in Mahican, a language so like our own Abenaki that I could understand them. Perhaps the white men were so worn by their long and hard journey that they hardly cared. Indeed, the words that two of the Rangers spoke to each other showed that they had little awareness of what went on about them.

"What be our savages a-talking about?" one of them said in a high, complaining voice.

"None of our business," the second one growled. "Long as they keeps a good watch and gets us vittles like this good vennyson, I'll not complain."

They all settled in around the fire, white Ranger and Stockbridge scout alike, eating their share of the venison my mother had roasted for them. None of them, not even the Stockbridge Indians, kept a careful watch now. But I knew that I would have no chance this night. They had set up their camp in a circle with the women in the center. I might slip by the white Rangers without rousing them, but the Stockbridges were another story. Their ears were as sharp as mine.

I settled in to watch and wait. The aroma of the meat, the first cooked meat I had smelled in days, made my mouth water. My stomach began to complain, growling so loudly that I was sure it could be heard at some distance. None of those about the fire heard it . . . or perhaps they simply thought the sound came from the porcupine.

They would not have been far from wrong. The animal had now made its way up to my hiding place on top of the hill. Apparently it was the porcupine's resting spot as well. After pressing its nose against mine to greet me and pulling on my hair with one of its paws, it curled up by my side. A porcupine is far from a pleasant companion for the night, but not one you can just push away. Such a push would be answered by a swift swipe from a well-armed tail. The one good thing about my unwanted companion was that he made it more certain I would not fall asleep. The possibility of rolling over onto a porcupine helps keep one wide awake.

24

THE MESSAGE

By the time morning arrived, I had made a plan. I waited until the party broke camp. The Stockbridge scouts were ready before dawn, but the white Rangers were not prepared to go until the sun was well up in the sky. When they were all out of sight and earshot, I rose and stretched myself. At some time in the night when I dozed off, my prickly sleeping companion had left me. None of his quills had pierced my flesh, but I did pluck a few from my leather leggings.

We were now on a part of the trail that would rise over the ridges to give a first long view of the great mountains on the other side of Petonbowk, Lake Champlain. Though it was a longer way to go, I turned onto another trail that would enable me to come out ahead of them. An old beech tree with the shape of an arrow carved into its side marked the cut-off. As soon as I was on the longer trail, I began to run.

I ran without stopping until the sun was in the middle of the sky, then finally paused at a sandy spring a few paces up-hill from the trail's bare stones. My mouth and throat were dry. I had the urge to thrust my head into the water and gulp like a wide-mouthed fish. But as I knelt to drink, what I saw in the sand made me smile. There, once again, were the tracks of a big wolf. My guardian was still watching out for me, reminding me to drink as a wolf drinks after it has been running. Slowly and sparingly. So I sipped a small mouthful, allowing the water to warm before swallowing it down. Too much cold water can make your belly cramp, es-pecially when you have eaten little and have far to run.

The sun was two hands past noon when I reached the main trail again. The trees thinned out here as the trail climbed over a high ridge. Hemlocks grew close to the trail's edge here too. I ran back along the path in the direc-tion from which the Rangers' party would be coming. At each turn in the trail as it climbed up through the hemlocks, I did as I had planned—once, twice, three times, four times, before turning back to the trail junction.

I found a place well up from the path where I could con-ceal myself among the stones. I waited. I waited longer. Their progress was slower than I had expected. The sun was only a hand's width from setting over the mountains on the other side of the lake when I heard them coming up the steep trail. Three of the Stockbridge scouts came first. The one named Jacob was in the lead, a musket cradled in his arms, a bow slung over his back. The Stockbridges were followed by the women and my two sisters. I could see that my mother and sisters seemed stronger than the other five women who were ahead of them. None of the other women were carrying anything. Clearly, my mother and my two sisters were being used like pack animals. Those five white women kept stumbling and often needed the attention of the two scouts behind Jacob. My mother and sisters, though they were obviously tired and heavily burdened, seemed sure on their feet.

Wli, I thought. Good. They are still strong enough to run.

Farther back the five Rangers straggled up the slope with Cheeksaunkun and one other Stockbridge behind them. It seemed as if the job that Cheeksaunkun and his friend had taken on was not just to watch their rear, but also to keep the exhausted white men moving.

I could see them all from my high vantage point, but my eyes were on my mother as she came to the first place I had chosen. I watched as her hand reached out, as if to catch herself from stumbling. Her quick fingers grasped the low, slender hemlock branch and untied the knotted circle I had left there. Then, as she continued on, she lifted her hand to tap her chest lightly.

She had seen my sign. She understood it so well that she had sent back a message, certain that a friend or relative was somewhere watching. It was a simple message, but it brought tears to my eyes. I knew she could not see or hear me, but I still tapped my heart lightly as I whispered, "My mother, I love you too."

I kept watching, though, to be certain. Sure enough, when she reached the next of the circled branches, she stopped to tighten her moccasin strings. Then she raised herself to her feet by grasping that very branch, and slipped free the knot with a quick pull.

I knew that she would speak to my sisters as soon as the opportunity presented itself. She would tell them that rescuers were close. Be ready for something. She would not tell the other women in the party, though. There was the chance that one of them might betray a rescue plan. Also, it would be far easier for three to escape than eight.

I felt pleased and allowed a small smile to shape itself on my face. The first part of my plan, to alert my mother and sisters, was working. It is always easier to help those who are aware that a savior is near. Then they will be prepared to act and not be frozen by surprise. Now, though, I had a problem. What was the second part of my plan? I was only one person, not a rescue party. What could I do now?

I placed one hand upon the sun-warmed earth and another upon the smooth old stone in front of me. The stone moved slightly as I leaned on it. Ah! I knew then what my plan would be. The land and the ancient stones would help me.

25

THE BEECH TREE

Although the Stockbridge scouts seemed to be the most able men in the small party, they were not the ones in charge. As I watched further, that became clear. The Ranger who wore the insignia of an officer was the one who called a halt shortly after I first saw them. I noted the looks that the scouts gave one another, but they did as he said. That officer was also the one who told them when to get moving again.

The ones who complained the most about being forced back on the trail were the five women. My mother and sisters just shouldered their packs and started walking, putting themselves ahead of the two lead Stockbridge scouts. I saw how Jacob watched my mother and nodded his head in approval of her strength. For some reason, it made me angry. I did not like seeing him look at my mother that way. I was close enough to hear his voice. The words he spoke made me even angrier.

"She is a little old," Jacob said, "but would make a good wife. I will see, when we get to Crown Point, if I can buy her. Our English brothers do not want her anyway. They are afraid that she will cut their throats as they sleep."

The other Stockbridge man laughed. "See how Sergeant Clark is still limping. It has been three full days since she kicked him."

Good for you, my mother, I thought.

As soon as the last of the party had passed, I began running to cut ahead of them through the forest. I hoped that the spot I was thinking of was still as I remembered it. I knew this might be my only chance to stage an ambush. When I reached the place, I was relieved. Not only was the trail steep and winding, but the big stones were there too. The crest of the hill fell away steeply, and a small trail on that other side led down through tangled brush to a valley. In the valley another narrower trail led through swampy ground to the Winooski River. The entrance to that second trail was hard to see, but my uncle had shown it to me when we passed through here a year ago. I was certain I could still find it, and I trusted that what he had shown me in the river was still there as well.

Near the start of the steepest climb, I found a perfect spot beside the main trail. It was dry now, but water from the last rains had pooled there, leaving a soft and sandy piece of ground the size of a large deerskin. I brushed it free of twigs and leaves, and bent over it with a sharp stick.

When I was done, I walked back down the trail a few feet to observe it. It was good. The eyes of a person climbing this trail with a burden on her back would be caught by what I had prepared. However, just to make sure, I piled seven small flat stones in the trail and wedged two sticks into them. The stones would stop a person's progress and the two sticks were like pointing fingers aimed at what I had scratched into the earth. They would also let my quick-thinking mother know who had left this message for her. Two Sticks.

Like me, my mother had learned to read. Usually she only read the Abenaki in the Bible translated by the Jesuits. But she also knew many words in the French language. I had written two of those words in that sandy place near the middle of the trail halfway up the hill. To draw her attention I had again left our sign by twisting a sapling branch into a circle. That first word, drawn in the earth at the base of the sapling, was *allez*. Go. It would tell her that she and my sisters must move even more quickly up the trail ahead of the others. The twisting arrow that I had drawn in the sand pointed to the second word: *riviere*. I trusted she would know I meant the Winooski River in the valley beyond and below.

This steep part of the trail was narrow, so narrow that no more than one person at a time could climb it. A still thinner deer path ran above it through the big old stones that were part of my plan. The deer path led to a spot even better than I had remembered. A wide-trunked old beech tree grew next to that path in just the right place. Its gray sides were covered with markings that looked like words in some language humans do not speak. Perhaps the claws of a bear marking its territory or of a bobcat climbing had made those marks. Or perhaps, as some say, the Little People leave messages for one another on such trees. I placed my hands on the tree and leaned my cheek against its cool bark.

Then, crouching down behind the old beech, I unslung my gun and pulled the tampion out of the end of the barrel. That small plug of wood was there to keep dirt and mud from falling into the musket. A musket with dirt in its barrel may blow up when it is discharged, killing the one who is trying to shoot it. I checked the flint, put in the powder from my horn, and used the ramrod to tamp in the wadding and the lead ball. Carefully I placed the gun behind the beech. I climbed a few paces up the slope directly behind the tree, stopping to look back now and then. I could not see the lower foot trail, which meant that my hiding place could not be seen by anyone on that trail. It was very good.

Finally, I went back down the hill along the deer path. The first of the line of balanced stones was only fifty paces down from the beech tree. There were three of those stones, each as large and round as a big barrel. Those stones had been here on this slope for a long time. Perhaps they were part of one of the Ancient Ones, the first people made by Ktsi Nwaskw. As the Great Mystery had hoped, those first people were very strong. But Ktsi Nwaskw had not been pleased with those first people. Their hearts were made of stone and they showed no respect for the rest of creation, crushing things beneath their heavy feet. So Ktsi Nwaskw broke them into smaller stones and scattered them across the land from the valleys to the highest hills.

It is strange what things come to you when you are about to go into battle. My uncle once told me that when he was fighting by the side of our brothers the French, he usually found himself thinking of games he played as a child. I found myself remembering the stories my mother used to tell me. One tale in particular came to me about Azeban the raccoon, the one who is always getting into trouble. As he is walking around one day, Azeban finds a great stone balanced on a hilltop.

"Grandfather," Azeban says to the stone, "have you been on this hilltop for a long time?"

"Grandson," the Great Stone replies, "I have always been here."

"I travel to many places," Azeban then says. "Would you like to travel, Grandfather?"

"Grandson," the Great Stone answers, "I do not think I would like to travel."

"Grandfather," Azeban says, with a smile on his face, "you are going to travel." Then he begins to push the big stone.

I would soon do the same. The dead tree limbs that I had wedged beneath each of the three boulders had already tipped them to the point where only one small push should be enough to start each of the stones rolling. I went to the one farthest down the deer path. Now all I had to do was wait.

26

WAITING

Strange as it may seem, considering the danger that lay ahead, the hardest part for me as I waited was staying awake. Perhaps it was because of all of the running, the long canoe travel, the lack of food, and the wound in my shoulder. Now that everything was ready, my body was finally telling me how much it needed rest.

I rubbed my eyes and shook my head. I could not slumber, not even for the length of a heartbeat. *Listen,* I said to myself. *Open your ears and listen. Hear what the forest has to say.*

The forest may seem quiet to one who walks through it without stopping. But that is because it is listening to us. When one sits in silence, the forest again finds its voice.

The first sound was that of *Mikoa magwajid,* the red squirrel, chirring and chirping from an oak tree upslope from me. Then I heard the rapid thumping near the top of a dead beech tree just below me. *Nobasas,* the pounder, was returning to his work of finding the little ones that bore beneath the bark. *Kejegigi, kejegigi,* a chickadee called, speaking its name in our language. With a flutter of wings, it landed on the closest branch of the small hemlock in front of me. It cocked its head at me and spoke again. *Kejegigi, kejegigi.*

Ti-de-so. A louder bird call came from far below near the base of the hill. It was the warning screech of the blue jay. *Ti-de-so. Ti-de-so.* With another flutter of its wings the chickadee was gone. Once again the forest held its breath. People were coming up the trail. All feelings of weariness left me.

I sucked in my lower lip and bit it as I watched and waited. I rubbed my Jesuit ring with my fingers. No matter how many plans one makes, one cannot guarantee success.

"In battle," Uncle Pierre told me, "the best plan is often the simplest one. Then there are fewer ways for it to go wrong."

I hoped my own plan was simple enough. But its success depended on several things: the laziness of the Bostoniak Rangers; the weakness of the other captive women; the arrogance of the Stockbridges, who were now certain they had far outdistanced any pursuer and so would be less watchful. Most of all, though, it depended upon the strength of my mother and my sisters. Their strength was the most important part of my plan.

The first person I saw was my little sister Katrin. The top of her head appeared for a moment around one of the bends and then vanished. Close behind her came Marie-Jeanne and then my mother. Just as I had hoped, they were ahead of all the others, even the Stockbridges. They moved with the smooth pace of those used to traveling great distances. Though it did not seem that they were hurrying, they were coming up the steep trail more quickly than one might usually make such a climb. It filled me with certainty that my mother had seen the signs I had left for her.

She and my sisters did not appear to be running away, yet the distance between them and the others was gradually growing.

I began to see more of the party. They were stretched out in a long line like the body of a snake. The person closest to my family, Jacob, was at least forty paces behind. He had turned and stopped to answer a question from a Bostoniak Ranger. From his limp and the insignia on his jacket, I knew that the white man was Sergeant Clark. Sergeant Clark was pointing down the hill. Just below him was another of the Rangers. Farther, much farther down, was the rest of the group. They were so far away that it was as if they were separate parties, as if the body of the snake had broken into pieces.

As steadily and strongly as my mother and sisters climbed, it seemed to take them forever to pass beneath me. I wanted to cry out and urge them to move faster, but I knew that would be a foolish thing to do. So much depended upon surprise. I could not give myself away yet. Katrin stumbled and fell forward on her hands, almost sliding off the trail itself. My mother grasped her by the shoulder, pulling her back and steadying her. Katrin's hands were scraped and bleeding, but she did not cry. She looked up at my mother and nodded. Marie-Jeanne tried to take Katrin's pack from her, but she shook her head. Then she turned and began to trudge up the trail again. My heart swelled with pride at my little sister's courage. I would not fail them.

At last they had passed below me and were safely up the trail. Jacob was now even farther behind them, still in conversation with Sergeant Clark. Jacob looked over his shoulder up the trail. I could see that he was not pleased. My mother and sisters were far ahead. Too far ahead. He turned, ready to run and catch up with them.

Now was the time. I pressed down on the tree limb wedged beneath the boulder. The boulder lifted slightly. It was almost ready to tip over and start tumbling down the slope. I pushed again, harder this time. With a sickening crack, the limb broke in half and the boulder settled back into place.

27

In Battle

In the moment that the branch cracked it seemed as if everything began to move as slowly as a stream clogged with winter ice. To my right I could see my mother and sisters heading up the trail. To my left and down the slope, Jacob, who had heard the cracking of the tree limb, was pulling his musket from his shoulder. Sergeant Clark was doing the same. And in my mind were more of my uncle's words. "Be prepared in battle, as there are many ways for even the simplest plan to go wrong."

Then I remembered. I *was* prepared. I reached back for the other tree limb I had placed behind me in case the first one broke. I shoved it beneath the boulder and leaned. The boulder rocked up. I pushed down again, less quickly than before, but with all my weight. The boulder tipped over with a thump and began to roll. It glanced off another stone and bounced up to strike the earth with a booming sound like the beat of a giant drum. It hit the tree that the redheaded pounder had been pecking, and the tree exploded as if it had been struck by a cannonball. Dead branches and great chunks of the trunk rained down onto the trail as Jacob and Sergeant Clark dove backward.

I heard people shouting from below as the stone continued down the slope. But I did not look back. I was at the second stone, prying with the branch wedged beneath it. This stone did not resist. Perhaps it had seen its brother flying down the hill and was eager to try the same thing. It went bounding down after the first one, crashing through brush and trees, dislodging other rocks as it went. Its own deep drumbeat echoed that of the first rolling boulder. The third stone did not fare as well as the first two. It rolled no more than a hundred paces before it split in half. But that started even more rocks rolling beneath it. The whole slope was moving. Trees fell. A large part of the trail vanished, sliding off to the side and then subsiding. It would not be easy for anyone to follow us now.

People were still shouting far below. I hoped that no one had been badly injured. It looked to me as if the stones had rolled not over the people but between the two halves of their party.

I began running up the slope again. Perhaps no one would follow, but I could not be certain of that. By now my mother and sisters would have reached the hilltop. They would have heard the sounds and begun running for the river. I was almost at the beech tree. I could see the markings on its bark with such clarity that I was almost able to read what they said.

But I did not reach the tree. Something like a sharp stone struck me in the side, twisting me down onto my back. As I fell, I heard the crack of the musket.

I was numb, but felt no pain. I looked down the slope in the direction of the sound of that shot. Fifty yards away, smoke was curling from the barrel of Sergeant Clark's musket. Jacob stood beside him, staring straight at me.

"Look to him," Clark shouted, motioning Jacob forward. "I'll see to the others." Then he turned and scrambled down the slope.

Jacob started climbing, his eyes on mine. I tried to move, but it was as if the strength had all been taken out of me. I was as weak as a baby rabbit watching the slow approach of a hungry fox. Jacob had put his musket down. He was now only a few paces away. His hand was on the hatchet at his belt. He would not waste a bullet on me.

Kat-a-chik!

It was the sound of a musket being cocked.

"Jannigobi," said a firm voice just behind me. "Stop walking and stand."

I knew that voice. It belonged to my mother. The gun I had hidden behind the tree was held up to her shoulder, aimed right at the Stockbridge scout.

Jacob stopped. He removed his hand from his hatchet

and stood straight. "Hunh?" he said, curling his lip as he spoke. Though my mother was pointing my gun at his chest, he was not about to show any fear. He looked down at me and then up at my mother.

"*Nianamon*," my mother said. "My son." She said it in such a way that it filled my heart and brought strength back into my limbs.

"*Nigawes*," I said to her, my eyes still on Jacob. "My mother." I pulled myself to my feet, using the tree trunk to steady me so that I could stand beside her.

Jacob looked at us. A smile came over his face and he shook his head. He tapped his left hand against his chest and then swung his arm outward. "Go," he said. Then he turned, as calmly as if he was simply out for a walk in the forest, and began to make his way down the hill. He went past the musket he had left behind him. Had he reached for it, I am certain that my mother would have shot him. Having seen the look in her eyes, I am certain that Jacob knew this as well as I did. We watched until he was out of sight.

"Your sisters are on the trail to the river," my mother said, her hands probing my side where the ball had struck me. She tore a piece of cloth from her long blouse and pressed it against the wound, tightening my belt to hold the compress in place. I was holding the musket now, looking down the slope. Perhaps Jacob had meant his gesture of respect; perhaps he really was telling us that we were free to go. Perhaps it was just a trick. In either case, this was no time to stop being watchful.

My mother stood back and looked up into my face. "Can you walk?" she asked.

My throat felt dry, but I managed to speak. *"Alosada,"* I said. "Let us go."

28

GOING HOME

We were only a short distance down the other side of the hill when my sisters met us. My mother had told them to make their way to the river and not turn back. They had done just the opposite. Katrin was in the lead. As always, she had made up her own mind about what to do. But neither my mother nor I was angry at them. Marie-Jeanne reached out to steady me with her hands. "My brother," she said, "thank you." Katrin stepped forward—without a word, which was strange for her—and put her arms around my waist. Smiling, my mother embraced the three of us. We four held one another in the circle of an embrace. All of our eyes were filled with tears.

We did not pause for long. We knew that these first moments of our escape were the most important ones. We had to move, move as quickly as we could.

By the time we reached the base of the slope, my strength was fading again. I leaned on the shoulders of my mother and Marie-Jeanne as we continued on. The entrance of the trail was just where I had remembered it. We pushed through the brush and found the hidden way through the swamp to the river.

I do not know how long it took. When I looked up at the sky to check the position of the sun, there was not one sun there but several. Then those several suns began to spin. I had to look back down at the earth to keep from falling. I forced my legs to keep moving. One step, then another. One step, then another. At last, when it seemed I could go no farther, I began to hear the sound of the river.

We came out onto the northern bank of the Winooski. Once again luck and memory were with me. The boat was there, only a spear's throw downriver. I waded into the water up to my waist. My mother followed. Together, we managed to roll out the stones that had held the dugout underwater. It bobbed slowly up to the surface. Carved out of the trunk of a single great aspen tree, the boat was about twenty feet long and wide enough to be stable. It is our practice to make such dugouts and hide them this way in distant places where we may need them for hunting or fishing. My father had made this one twelve winters ago. The four of us managed to get it to the bank and tip it to drain the remaining water out of it.

While my mother and I had been removing the stones, Marie-Jeanne and Katrin had been finding poles. We would be going downstream and did not need paddles. The long poles could be used to guide our boat by thrusting them against the bottom in shallow places and pushing off from the rocks and the banks of the river.

I sat down on a large flat stone by the riverbank. It had been warmed by the sun. That is why I became drowsy. I leaned back and kept leaning. I heard my head strike the stone, but I did not feel anything. Darkness closed its arms around me like a great cloud embracing the sky.

The next thing I knew, someone was calling my name. It was hard to open my eyes. When I did so, I saw the faces of my mother and my sisters looking down at me. I tried to answer them, but my mouth had forgotten how to make words. My eyes closed again.

"Help me carry him," I heard my mother say. Her voice was very far away. It was the last thing I heard for a long time.

I remember nothing of the journey we made down the Winooski. I have only the memories of my sisters and my mother to rely upon.

The journey took a day and a night. We stopped only once, in a sheltered inlet at an old abandoned village site. There my mother and sisters carried me from the canoe and made a fire. My mother made a soup and spooned it into my mouth. Though I do not recall it at all, she said I was very hungry and asked for more.

"You were as weak as a little chipmunk," Katrin told me later.

"Hah," Marie-Jeanne added. "No chipmunk ever weighed

as much as you do. I thought my back would break when we had to carry you."

We could go no farther than the big falls. From that point on we had to walk. Again, I have no recollection of that part of the journey. Somehow my feet seemed to know what to do on their own and kept me moving. We came at last to Petonbowk, Lake Champlain, at a place where one can look out from a bluff and see the island of Odzihozo. He is the ancient one who shaped the lake long ago and then turned himself into stone so that he could always remain there in that beautiful place. I have no memory of our standing together on that high bluff, although my mother and my sisters all insist that I spoke a prayer of thanksgiving as we looked out over the wide water.

What I do recall are the people who helped us. My first clear memory is of waking in a bed, a real bed in a room made of logs and planks. Warmth came from the fireplace across the room. A white man and a white woman stood near the bed talking with my mother. Their voices sounded kind to me. My two sisters were seated on the plank floor with a small blonde-haired boy, the three taking turns spinning a top.

My mother and the man and woman turned to look down at me.

"My son," my mother said, "you are awake."

"I am," I tried to answer. What came from my mouth sounded like the caw of a raven.

The white man put his slender hand on my forehead.

"No need for thee to talk," he said. He tapped my right hand, which lay on my chest. "Open thy hand."

I opened my hand and he placed something in it that was small and heavy and round. I managed to raise my hand to look at it. It was a musket ball.

"I took it from thy side," he said. "Thou shalt heal up fine now."

"*Wliwini,*" I croaked. "Thank you."

"Thank the Lord," the woman said.

I must have gone back to sleep. When I opened my eyes again, I did so with ease and I was able to sit up. The man and woman, my sisters, and the boy were all gone. My mother, though, was sitting on the floor near the foot of the bed. She nodded at me.

"Where are we?" I said.

"We are still near Petonbowk," she said. "These white people are friends." Then she smiled. "There is no winter in their hearts."

From that moment on, my memories are clear. I remember the three remaining days we stayed there while my strength returned. I remember the morning when we left the cabin of the Bedell family. Their son, Timothy, had placed his top in the hands of my sister Katrin. We did not say good-bye or look back to wave at them. That is not our way of taking leave of friends. I kept their kindness in my heart, knowing that I would see them again. I would find some way to repay them for all they had given with no thought of gaining anything in return.

From there our journey back home was uneventful. Strangely, though, part of our route was the same as that taken by the Bostoniak Rangers on their way to attack our village. When we reached Missisquoi, our Abenaki cousins there showed us—with some amusement—the supplies and canoes that the Rangers had tried to hide in their swamps. They gave us a good store of those Bostoniak supplies for our use on the way home. We crossed overland to the place where I had hidden my canoe. Then, after passing through Lake Memphremagog, the rest of the way home to St. Francis was downriver.

By the time we reached our village, a full month had passed since that terrible day. Part of my mind hoped, as we traveled, that I would wake one morning to realize that all of the awful events had been no more than a bad dream. I would wake to find the half circle of houses and cabins intact. I would hear the bell ringing from the church.

But, of course, it had not been a dream. What I saw was much as I remembered. The smells of smoke and blood and fear were gone. But so, too, was our village. Only those same three buildings remained standing among the blackened ruins of our homes. The few families who had stayed in and around St. Francis welcomed us elatedly. All rejoiced that my mother and sisters had been saved. Among them were the Worrier and my uncle Pierre, who had returned a week before us. Since his return, he and the Worrier had constructed a bark lodge for our family to live in.

"White Man Talker will bring them back," the Worrier had told my uncle. "They must have a place to stay."

Knowing better than to question him, my uncle had set to work.

Uncle Pierre told us of those who had gone to live at other mission villages or to winter over in their hunting grounds. He showed us the burial place for the thirty who had died in the raid, most of them women and children.

When my uncle and I were alone, I wrapped my arms around him in a strong warrior's embrace. As I did so, I noticed for the first time that my head was now above his.

"My uncle," I said, "I thank you for all you have taught me."

He grasped me by the upper arms and shook me gently. "My sister's son," he said. That was all.

29

THE CIRCLE WITHIN THE CIRCLE

So it was that I brought my family home. I saved them and they saved me. Nothing that I did was done alone. I was helped by so many along the way: the teachings of my parents and my uncle, the Worrier and my great-grandfather Beaver's Tail; the kindness of the white people in their cabin near Petonbowk; even one of our enemies, the Stockbridge warrior Jacob, who showed his respect for our courage by sending us on our way. I was helped, too, by the animal people, the waters, and the stones. I was helped by this land that loves us because we keep the summer in our hearts.

But this story was not yet ended, though I did not know it on the day when I embraced my uncle and thanked him. Moons passed, and new homes were built on the ruins of St. Francis not far from the graves that held the bodies of those who had died. Perhaps one of those graves held the body of brave Piel, as some were too badly burned for us to identify. My dear friend Piel was never seen again.

A new church began to rise from the ruins of the old one. A new priest came to live among us and lead us in our prayers for the souls of those who were lost. He took the place of Father Roubaud—whose shame led him to seek another place. Chief Gill, whose heart would never allow him to desert St. Francis, was hard at work on a new home that would be even finer than his first one.

Then, on a bright summer afternoon, a young man wearing the clothing of a white man came walking into St. Francis. Marie-Jeanne and I were the first to notice him, even before his father did. His face was worn by his ordeal, but he was still as handsome as ever. It was Antoine Gill.

Antoine and I thrust our hands out to grasp each other by the wrists in the old way that we always shook hands. Marie-Jeanne stroked his shoulder with her palms, her face wearing a smile so wide that I thought her head would split.

"My friend," I said.

"My friend," he answered. "I have so much to tell you. Our sister Mrs. Johnson sends you her love."

Then Antoine told me his tale. The retreat from St. Francis had been a hard one for the Bostoniak Rangers and their captives. His mother and brother had not been killed and eaten, but died when both fell off a cliff. Rogers had seen that their bodies were buried and ordered heavy stones to be piled over the graves to keep away animals.

Antoine had been chosen by the White Devil Rogers himself to be their guide down the Connecticut River. It was a journey that Antoine had made before in the company of his father. After many long and hard days of travel, they had reached Fort Number Four. During that time Antoine had learned to respect Rogers, even if he had no love for him. In return, Rogers had given his young guide into the care of an English family that had taken up residence near the fort in Charlestown.

"Imagine my surprise," Antoine told me, "when I walked into that house and saw her face. 'Mon Dieu,' I shouted, 'it is my sister, it is my sister Susannah!'" Antoine laughed with delight. "And my older sister Mrs. Susannah Johnson was no less pleased to see me. She asked me to send her love and good thoughts to everyone she remembers—especially you, Saxso, and your family."

It is strange the circles that our lives make. I said so this morning to the Worrier. In response he traced a circle in the sand and then drew another within it.

"We are always within the eye of the Creator," he said. "Wherever we look, we will find that each is connected to the other. Only those who live with the winter in their hearts cannot see those connections. We must not hate those Winter People, White Man Talker. Pity them. Keep the summer in your heart."

I shall try to do just that.

AUTHOR'S NOTE

Along the banks of the St. Francis River in the province of Quebec is the small Abenaki village of Odanak that was itself once named St. Francis. During the eighteenth century it was a place of some importance. Global conflict between England and France had forced millions of people belonging to many nations to declare their allegiance to one or another of the two great Colonial powers. Strongly allied with the French, St. Francis Abenaki war parties went south again and again to strike in guerilla raids at the heart of what had become known as New England. Although the Indian warriors of St. Francis were few—never more than 150 men at any given time—their name was feared.

In October of 1759 an event occurred that changed everything for the Abenakis. Major Robert Rogers led a force of 200 men, some of whom were Stockbridge Indian scouts, in an attack on St. Francis. Here is how Rogers summarized the action in dispatches sent in November of 1759 to General Jeffrey Amherst:

Half an hour before sunrise we surprised the village, approaching it in three divisions, on the right, left, and centre; which was effected with so much caution and promptitude on the part of the officers and men that the enemy had no time to recover themselves, or to take arms in their own defence, until they were mostly destroyed. Some few fled to the water; but my people pursued, sunk their canoes, and shot those who attempted to escape by swimming. We then set fire to all the houses except three, reserved for the use of our party.

The fire consumed many Indians who had concealed themselves in their cellars and house-lofts, and would not come out. At seven o'clock in the morning the affair was completely over. We had by that time killed two hundred Indians, and taken twenty women and children prisoners. Fifteen of the latter I suffered to go their own way, and brought home with me two Indian boys and three girls. Five English captives were also found, and taken into our care.

When the detachment paraded, Captain Ogden was found to be badly wounded, being shot through the body, but still able to perform his duty. Six privates were wounded and one Stockbridge Indian killed.

It was only one of many English victories celebrated during what the English later called "the year of miracles," a year that would end with English domination of the North American continent. However, the attack on St. Francis was of great symbolic importance to the English and achieved legendary status in the years that followed. The Abenakis, Major Rogers reported, were wiped out. Indeed, from that point on, the Abenakis never again posed a significant military threat to the American colonies.

Beret-wearing Rangers entered the pages of military history with their raid on St. Francis. To this day, Rogers' Rangers are held up as the prototypes of the Green Berets and other small elite military units operating behind enemy lines. Rogers himself would continue to attract attention, not only as a soldier, but as an explorer in his search for a nonexistent northwest water route across North America. Ironically, he became known in London as a playwright whose theme was the nobility of the American Indian. In the twentieth century the romance of Rogers and his famous raid would be further immortalized in the novel *Northwest Passage* by Kenneth Roberts. In the popular movie of that same name, Rogers, played by Spencer Tracy, reports that the Abenakis have been totally exterminated.

The Abenaki version of the story, a side now being borne out by modern historians, is quite different. The people of St. Francis, a relatively new village built around a stone church, were refugees and survivors of previous massacres by the English. By 1759, many Abenakis lived in homes and wore clothing much like that of their French neighbors. The majority of Abenakis had been raised as Roman Catholics and were ardent churchgoers. When Abenaki raiders, acting in alliance with the French, struck at New England, those Indians were returning home to lands that had been theirs only a few decades before. Yet the primary desire of the majority of the Abenaki people was to live in peace. Only a few years before the events of 1759 they had been trading and cooperating with the Bostoniak (the Abenaki name for the English and the American colonists), even though this displeased their French allies. Then several Abenaki tribal leaders were murdered by Englishmen, and war began again.

Contrary to the reports later filed by Robert Rogers, his raid was less successful than he claimed. The St. Francis Abenaki were far from wiped out. At most, only a third of its inhabitants—mostly women, children, and old people—were in Odanak when the attack took place. According to Abenaki oral history, they were warned just before the attack by one of the Indian scouts accompanying Rogers. Most slipped away before the attack happened. No more than twenty or thirty Abenakis were killed. Then as Rogers and his Rangers retreated, the Bostoniak were pursued and attacked by the Abenakis. As Rogers himself reports, the white attackers suffered severe casualties—about a third of Rogers' Rangers lost their lives during their disastrous retreat, either due to vengeful Abenakis or starvation. The village of Odanak was rebuilt. With the departure of the French, the Abenakis then found themselves in a new relationship with their former enemies. They became trading partners with the Bostoniak, and their warriors were courted by both the English and the Americans during the Revolutionary War.

Some Abenakis quietly returned to parts of their homelands in New England or remained in relatively isolated communities in northern Vermont, New Hampshire, and New York. They lived peacefully, but it was painful to hear the way their history was recorded. As one history book used in Vermont until the 1970's put it, they were the "bloody St. Francis Indians who were exterminated by Rogers' Raid." I still find recently published books in which the Abenakis are described as "an extinct tribe."

For many years I thought of writing about the events of Rogers' Raid. It was, in part, a personal thing. My own great-grandfather Louis Bowman was born in St. Francis. The Bedell family, white people who later married in among the Abenakis, are among my wife's ancestors. Also, the untold or misinterpreted events of history have long fascinated me, not just in American Indian history, but around the world. Things are so often only heard from one side. It has led me in the past to write such books as *The Arrow Over the Door* and *Sacajawea,* whose dual narrators represent quite different personal and cultural viewpoints. About twenty years ago various members of my family and I began to reconnect with St. Francis. We visited, took part in festivals, and listened to elders. Some of them, like Cecile Wawanolette, were direct descendants of survivors of Rogers' Raid and could relate, in Abenaki, tales about the events of that awful night. My younger son, Jesse, spent months at Odanak, talking and working with Cecile and others as he put together a syllabus for teaching Abenaki, a language threatened with extinction because there are now fewer than a hundred fluent speakers, most over the age of fifty. The work of my dear friend the late Gordon Day, an anthropologist who devoted his life to Abenaki studies, was invaluable. (With the help of Jeanne Brink, herself a descendant of Rogers' Raid survivors, Day compiled and saw into print the largest dictionary ever put together of any American Indian language.) Gordon was the first to write in depth about the Indian oral traditions related to Rogers' Raid, and I have returned again and again to his work with gratitude.

By the time I began *The Winter People,* I was far from short of documentation. There is at least as much history in this story as there is fiction. Most of the people I mention by name in the novel are real. Even those few of my characters who are fictional—my protagonist, his family, and the Worrier—are based on historical figures and events. Two of the more fascinating "real people" in my story are Joseph-Louis Gill and Mrs. Suzanne Willard Johnson. Known as "The White Chief of the St. Francis Abenaki," Joseph-Louis was the son of Samuel Gill, a white child who had been captured by the Abenakis near Salisbury, Massachusetts, in June 1697 at the age of ten. Taken to St. Francis, Samuel Gill was adopted, baptized as a Roman Catholic, and brought up as an Indian. Around 1715 he married another adopted white captive, whose white name is recorded only as "Miss James." The oldest of their seven children, Jeanne-Magdeleine, was born in 1715 and married Hannis (probably Johannes), a German who also had been taken captive and adopted by the Abenakis. Joseph-Louis, born in 1719, was Samuel's oldest son. His marriage to Nanamaghemet, whose baptismal name was Marie-Jeanne, the daughter of a prominent Abenaki chief, probably raised his status in the community as much as his highly publicized exploits as a fierce warrior. Five feet ten inches tall and blonde-haired, he was elected as a *Sogmo* after serving in the French campaign against the Miami Indians in 1747—when he ate the heart of that hapless rattlesnake!

It was in Chief Gill's household that Suzanne Johnson found herself after she was taken captive. Although some white people were adopted into the tribe, most had an experience like Mrs. Johnson's, living in a relatively unpleasant form of servitude for some time before being either ransomed back by their families or absorbed into the French community. (Unlike the English colonies, where there was no shortage of white people, French colonies around the world always had fewer European immigrants, were much more likely to intermarry with indigenous people, and were eager to absorb new blood.) White captivity narratives were the best-sellers of their day. The book written by Mrs. Johnson after her own ransom was paid, *A Narrative of Mrs. Johnson's Captivity Among the French and Indians,* was extremely popular. She did, indeed, take in Antoine Gill after the St. Francis Raid. Antoine later went on to attend Dartmouth College (which had as its original much-neglected mission the education of New England Indians).

I've been told by some of my Abenaki friends who've read this story in manuscript that it is the most important thing I've ever written. However, I'm not vain or foolish enough to think that it is more than just a story. The survival against all odds of the Abenaki people and the traditions that are still passed from generation to generation are far more important than anything I've ever done. I only hope that some readers may be moved and informed by this book. I hope my work may help some realize, as I have been taught by my Abenaki elders, how necessary it is to always keep the summer in our hearts.

ACKNOWLEDGMENTS

First I must mention my family—my wife, Carol, for her strength and her belief in my work and our people; my sons, Jesse and Jim, for their devotion to sharing the language and the traditional ways; my sister Marge for her tireless pursuit of the truth behind our stories.

Some of my friends and teachers have passed on and now walk the Road of Stars. But I see them and hear their voices as I write this. There is Maurice Dennis, whose Abenaki name, Mdawelasis, Little Loon, reminds me of the way he always dove down to find that which was hidden but needed to be brought to the light. There is Stephen Laurent, Abenaki linguist and historian. One of the gentlest and kindest of men, he advised not only me but also Kenneth Roberts. (I recall Stephen saying to me, a bit wistfully, that he wished Mr. Roberts had listened a little better.) There is, of course, Gordon Day, whose words I have returned to again and again. I imagine that he and Stephen and the good old men he recorded, such as Ambrose Obomsawin and Adrian Panadis, are talking in Abenaki and laughing together even now in that place where the berries are always ripe. There is Chief Blackie Lampman, who tried hard to find that way of balance between the white and the Indian worlds. Molly Keating, who remembered her family's stories and worked even when she was ill to bring the hearts of the people together. There is Chief Homer St. Francis, who lived as a warrior in a country that seldom understood the love for Ndakinna, Our Land, that still lives in Abenaki souls. There is Wolf Song, who shared the stories and the pain of being Abenaki in this age, and whose ashes dance the wind above Snake Mountain.

Jeanne Brink gave me permission to retell the true story of her ancestor Obomsawin's rescue of Malian, the little girl left behind, and to include her song, which is still sung by the Obomsawin family. Patrick Cote, the director of the Musée des Abénakis in Odanak, was a constant source of information and was one of many in the Abenaki community who read my manuscript and offered helpful criticism. John Moody and Donna Roberts are among my dearest and best friends. Their generosity and knowledge have been a blessing, not just to my life but to all those who have been touched by them and their work to bring the bones of the ancestors back to rest, to cleanse our land for the generations to come.

Louis Annance, Cheryl Bluto, Alanis Obomsawin, Rick Obomsawin, Tom Obomsawin, April St. Francis, Fred Watso, Fred Wiseman, Aaron York . . . There are so many Abenaki people whose work and words are a continued blessing. *Wliniwi.* As many as I think to list, I know there are more who have touched me and influenced my writing and deserve to be mentioned. I ask that they forgive me for anything and anyone I may have forgotten. *Wli dogo wôngan.* All my relations. *Wlipamkaani, nidobak.* Travel well, my friends.

J
FIC
BRU

Bruchac, Joseph,
1942-

The winter people.

33910010317288
$16.99   Grades 4-6   10/28/2002

DATE			

004234   9487656